The Glasgow Collection

Glasgow 1999
UK City of
Architecture
and Design

Published on behalf of Glasgow 1999: UK City of Architecture and Design, by:

August
116–120 Golden Lane
London EC1Y OTL
+44 171 689 4400
mail@augustmedia.co.uk

© 1999 August Media Ltd

ISBN: 1 902 854 05 5

This work is subject to copyright. All rights are reserved, whether the whole or part of the material is concerned, specifically the rights of translation, reprinting, re-use of illustrations, recitation, broadcasting, reproduction on microfilms or in other ways, and storage in data banks. For any kind of use permission of the copyright owner must be obtained.

Cover photograph:
Balsa, a new Glaswegian bar, features a Glasgow Collection product, the *Chasm* chair designed by One Foot Taller.
© Keith Hunter

Photography:
David Churchill; pages 62, 63
Alan Dimmick, pages 20–21
Robert Perry, page 25
David Spero; pages 6–15
Chris Tubbs, pages 65–69

Series editor: Sarah Gaventa, Communications Director, Glasgow 1999
Editor: Nick Barley
Copy editors: Alex Stetter, Jessica Lack
Art director: Stephen Coates
Designer: Anne Odling-Smee
Editorial assistant: Jonathan Heaf

Contributors:
Bruce Wood
Simon Paterson
Sarah Paterson
Richard Seymour
Fiona Bradley
Texts © the authors

Production co-ordinated by Uwe Kraus GmbH
Colour separations by Fotolito Garbero, Italy
Printed in Italy by Musumeci

Preface
4
Deyan Sudjic, director of Glasgow 1999, Stuart Gulliver, director of the Glasgow Development Agency and Alastair Colquhoun of the Royal Bank of Scotland

Products of the City
6
A photographic essay by David Spero showing the Glasgow Collection in its urban context

The Glasgow Collection
16
Bruce Wood, director of the Glasgow Collection project, explains the thinking behind the project

A new kind of brand
22
An analysis of the successes of the project by brand consultants Simon and Sarah Paterson

Catalogue of the Collection
26
Alex Stetter

Case study 1 Ursula bath
36
Richard Seymour

Case study 2 Linnklok wrist watch
46
Philip Tolan

Case study 3 Please Touch
64
Fiona Bradley

Preface

The key aim of the Glasgow Collection is to showcase Glasgow's intrinsic design capability by generating creative, high value products, which are internationally competitive, and promote stronger links between the city's manufacturers and designers. The process that the Glasgow Collection has established – to assess, encourage, and develop new design ideas – has been nationally recognised as a 'best practice' model for design development and the Collection has been awarded Millennium Products status by the Design Council.

Design is a high value-added economic activity. It takes ideas, concepts and raw market data and through a creative process, produces world-beating products and services. It is a key source of non-price competition and permits business to create differentiated products.It is in the area of non-price competition that countries like Scotland will increasingly have to compete since price advantages, to a large extent, have been eroded. In the 'knowledge economy' where the emphasis is on content, designers are part of the intellectual capital of the economy and therefore an important aspect of the competitive advantage within it.

Being competitive through value-added design activity requires a higher level of design sophistication whether this is through ergonomics, functionality, decoration or symbols. This level of sophistication is a measure of the society in which a product has been created and its success is borne out by the demand for it. The Glasgow Collection has greatly contributed to raising this level of sophistication in Glasgow, and through the design and manufacture of the Collection, it has generated new consumer demand.

The Glasgow Collection has proved that design is a key element in any economy, creating dynamism and driving economic performance. The Glasgow Collection will form a sound foundation for continued growth in design in Glasgow, confirming the city's design capability nationally and internationally and as a fitting legacy of Glasgow 1999: UK City of Architecture and Design.

Stuart Gulliver, Chief Executive, Glasgow Development Agency

The Royal Bank of Scotland has a long and well documented history of sponsoring a range of projects in both Scotland and England, The arts world including theatre, dance, art and music; the sports world including rugby, golf, swimming and badminton; community projects such as mileposts for the national cycle network and ways of tackling social exclusion; and educational projects such as computers for schools and financial education, have all been recent recipients of the of the Royal Bank's extensive sponsorship and community programme.

Another area of great importance to us is the development of small to medium sized businesses. Hence our support of the Glasgow Collection. With over 300,000 small business customers, the Royal Bank knows how important it is for new start-ups and fledgling businesses to have access to the advice and encouragement they need to develop.

The first step in developing a business is a good idea it goes without saying that design is one of the means by which a good idea can most obviously manifest itself. However, seeing the practical advantages – and disadvantages – of some seemingly great designs, developing their potential, seeking financial and other backing, going into production, developing markets, finding retail opportunities and preparing long term business plans, almost without exception require external help and expertise. The Glasgow Collection has proved itself to be a model in this respect.

The Royal Bank's support of the Glasgow Collection has enabled the further development of over a dozen designs so far. Some designers have used our support to develop a much-needed prototype, some have used it to develop tools to make the prototype, and others have used it to take the prototype to design and product fairs all over the UK and Europe.

The Royal Bank's involvement has been gratifying on a number of counts – without our support many of the success stories in this book would not have happened; it has also been gratifying to see so many innovative design and business ideas, innovation being a key element of the Bank's philosophy. Finally, we are always keen to add our support to projects in Glasgow and the west of Scotland and to have been associated with one of the many successes of Glasgow 1999.

Alastair Colquhoun, Regional Retail Director, Royal Bank of Scotland

Foreword

Deyan Sudjic, Director
Glasgow 1999

There is a long history of attempts by well meaning officialdom to intervene in the design process, dating back to at least the Great Exhibition of 1851. Prince Albert's biggest concern in staging the event was the worrying notion that Britain's manufacturers were being overtaken by the French, the Germans and the Austrians. The exhibition provided a showcase for the best of what Britain was capable of, and also brought home to Britain what its competitors were capable of. In 1951, the Festival of Britain had less emphasis on foreign production, but still attempted to act as a stimulus to British design, in much the same way as the recently established Design Council was doing, with a blend of patrician good taste and exhortation.

In the 1980s the Thatcher government also discovered design, which it saw primarily as a means of assisting hard pressed domestic industries to fight off Japanese imports. The trouble with such an approach is that while design is of course a reflection of manufacturing strength, it is also a form of cultural expression. It is not only about the optimisation of the manufacturing process, it is also a way for an individual to express the values that are important to them. It is a reflection of the way we live. And it is with this in mind that the Glasgow Collection was established as a fundamental aspect of Glasgow's year as UK City of Architecture and Design.

With the financial support of the Glasgow Development Agency and the Royal Bank of Scotland, Glasgow 1999 set out to create a range of innovative product designs, some of which would have immediate commercial applications, others which would be aimed more at long term research, but all of which would have resonances with the wider public. The idea was to make the most of design talent within Glasgow, but also of the manufacturing possibilities within the city, to come up with a series of innovative and engaging pieces of product design. It was envisaged that it would have the effect of supporting young designers, setting out to make their first steps in the market place. And it has been very encouraging to see over the last three years how well the Glasgow designers involved with the collection have done, winning scores of prizes and attracting attention from all over the world. At the same time the intention was to give Glasgow manufacturers, from sheet metal workers to high tech electronics companies, the benefit of the best design advice from around the world. Gratifyingly this has also happened. And because the whole process has been geared up to realising actual products rather than abstract concepts, there is now an enormously impressive body of work to show. It has been a unique experiment, one that has proved hugely successful in meeting its objectives.

Argyll
Furnishing Fabrics
House Light Family
Low
Coffee Table
Pup
Furniture Range

The Lighthouse, Viewing platform
Pup
Furniture Range
Yo-Yo
Table

Three-legged Chair
Quentin
Paper pulp lamp

Kelvingrove Park
Skins
Digital Drum
Bone China Lamp

Alexandra Park golf course

Snowster
Snowboard
robbo
Robbo
Neck Guard

The Lighthouse, balcony
Hot metal
Cooking plate
Amulet
Map
Paperclip

Spirit level
Baby feed spoon
Chankey
Chankey

The Lighthouse, temperature control storage vault

Esk
Office System
Coffee Counter
Chair
Furniture Range
SIMPLY COMPUTERS
SHARP

The Glasgow Collection is a unique initiative created to promote innovative design in Glasgow, and to raise the city's profile as a design centre throughout Scotland and the UK. It has funded the design of over 50 new products, taken them to prototype stage, and promoted them to an international audience. *Bruce Wood*

In a period of less than three years, the Glasgow Collection has brought together designers from Glasgow, as well as from the rest of Scotland and outside the country, bringing a number of the prototypes into production, working with local manufacturers and helping to create well-designed products which are making local businesses more competitive.

The strategy

Early in 1995 it was announced that Glasgow had won the competition to become UK City of Architecture and Design 1999, and that Deyan Sudjic was to be its director. A key ingredient in Glasgow's recipe for success was design, and following on from the results of two independent reports investigating the economic standing of Glasgow commissioned by the Glasgow Development Agency, the idea for the Glasgow Collection was developed. An opportunity was recognised for a project that would both help local manufacturers utilise design and diversify and also give young designers coming out of college the chance to have some of their ideas realised in Glasgow. The Glasgow Collection was set up to make that infrastructural link happen. With three years available to us, the comparatively quick development of industrial design objects offered Glasgow an opportunity to make a real international impact as early as 1997, and to continue to build awareness until the project's climax in 1999. We pledged that each year, 15 products would be developed to prototype stage with the assistance of the Glasgow Collection, leading to 45 in total. These would be exhibited in a major exhibition at the end of 1999, and with luck, many of them might even have been taken into full-scale production.

Equally importantly, the Glasgow Collection needed to go beyond simply helping the local design community: the Collection had to have a theme, and it did not take long for one to emerge. Throughout its history, the city of Glasgow has attracted inventors, entrepreneurs and innovators, and it seemed apt to continue the aims of invention and innovation in the Collection. Each product must feature a truly innovative element, whether in previously untested use of materials, a new way of functioning, or even an innovative partnership between people who would not otherwise have worked together.

The key players

When we started working on the Glasgow Collection on 1 July 1997, the funding for the project was in place – financial support from the Glasgow Development Agency amounting to a combined total of around £750,000 – but there were no rules and no precedent to draw upon: simply the basic target of 45 new projects, of which 15 should go into production. By thinking about what would be most useful to the designers, one of the key decisions of the project was made: there would be no application forms, there would be dialogue instead. Each project was assessed on its own merits: we would meet, look at ideas, discuss the work and bring in other people to the project as necessary. While the money and time allocated to each project varied, individual legally binding contracts were negotiated with everyone involved. But there was something still lacking: far from wanting to be a simple grant-making organisation, the Collection needed to provide business and strategic consultancy to young designers, and we needed a partner who could help us offer this. Demonstrating considerable courage, flexibility and an acceptance of risk, the Royal Bank of Scotland agreed to sponsor the project. Their assistance included business loans at competitive rates, financial advice, and in-kind sponsorship of many of the projects. These grants were given to start-up companies and those without access to another revenue stream. It was a far-sighted move by the bank, generating enormous good will from a community of designers who could form an important generator of income for Glasgow in the future, as long as sufficient work could be generated to prevent a brain drain of designers from the city.

Next, we assembled a panel of independent advisers whose consultancy would help us keep in mind the bigger picture at all times. It was essential that the panel should be chosen for its experience in making links between designers and manufacturers, as well as having a good knowledge of industrial design in general. The advisory group consisted of:

• Simon Paterson, a corporate identity and strategic planning consultant. With many years' experience of product design projects for international clients, Paterson undertook research and planning required to identify partners in the manufacturing sector located in the Glasgow region. Paterson's six-month research exercise played a key role in the project, and helped to identify a number of manufacturers which subsequently became involved in Glasgow Collection projects.

• James Woudhuysen, whose experience at the design group Fitch, then as a predictor of trends at the Henley Centre for Forecasting during the 1980s, and at the Dutch manufacturing giant Philips, brought further breadth of experience to the group. Woudhuysen's recent move to the industrial design group Seymour Powell as a trends analyst had given him important experience of working in close association with designers.

• Sebastian Conran of Sebastian Conran Associates, another internationally-renowned product designer.

• A representative of the Glasgow Development Agency was invited to provide advice on the specific needs of Glasgow and its design and manufacturing organisations.

• Our other key supporter, the Royal Bank of Scotland, was represented by Alastair Colquhoun.

• Paul Copland of Scottish Design was invited in order to provide important strategic advice relating to design in Scotland.

• The panel was completed by Tim Wilkinson, an independent economist.

Selecting projects

The structure of the Collection was now in place, and we set about the task of identifying potential projects. At first, we had to make most of the running; there was little culture of mutual support among designers in the city, and although much innovative thinking was going on, many of the designers living there had become accustomed to a lifestyle of scavenging for small-scale commissions, producing products on a hand-made, one-off basis in their studios. Making the leap to the philosophy of larger-scale production was bound to take time. Equally, it would have been easy to throw away vast amounts of money on projects with no hope of financial success – but our budget had to see us through 50 designs, and three years of hard work.

We decided to start out with a small number of ideas already in development. A stainless steel bath by the Glasgow-based company Submarine was proposed; and we partnered the designers (who, astonishingly, had previously only produced graphic design work) with the local firm Associated Metal, whose work had previously involved the manufacture of such prosaic objects as vandal-proof toilets for prisons and mortuary slabs. It was an inventive piece of partnering, and the result was an award winner. Another designer, Glasgow graduate Ben Smith, was developing a digital drum machine with a user-friendly interface. The Collection offered help in translating the idea into a manufacturable design, and put Smith and his collaborator David Bernard in touch with a London-based manufacturer. The product is now fully functional and ready for sale. With these and several other early ideas, the process of building a design collection was under way.

In some cases, the project funding paid for the design element, in others was a practical contribution, making tooling or production possible. We also supported conceptual projects that would otherwise not have happened and gave students and graduates opportunities to learn by turning their ideas into reality.

Of course, not every idea we were presented with was suitable for the Collection – not because they were not good, just not right for us: the Glasgow Collection is essentially design-led, it is about domestic products and helping manufacturers, not jet engines and microchips. Nevertheless, all the projects that were chosen received guidance and practical support as well as funding.

Over the following 18 months, we worked on the development of a further 15 products. In each case, the Collection weighed up the design proposal, offered consultancy on the design and manufacturability if the project was deemed to be suitable, and helped to establish partnerships with manufacturers for a large number of them. Towards the middle of 1998 the fruits of our labours really began to pay off. With news of the Glasgow 1999 project in general spreading throughout Europe, and knowledge of the Glasgow Collection in particular spreading rapidly among designers in Scotland and elsewhere, the number of proposals began to increase rapidly; the overall quality and levels of innovation steadily improved.

Bute Fabrics, the company based on the eponymous west coast island and whose textiles are among the best respected for contract upholstery, offered to participate in a project to work with the designer Jasper Morrison on the development of a series of 1999 fabrics. Scottish manufacturer Linn Products, led by the forward-thinking Ivor Tiefenbrun, engaged Richard Seymour to work on the design of a new watch. And Scottish design retailer Nice House, headed up by Andy Harrold, began work on the development of an all-plastic dining chair with the emerging design partnership One Foot Taller.

Many of the products in the Collection are objects designed for the home; lights, chairs, clocks and a bathtub, reflecting a significant rise in home ownership over the past 20 years. Another key category is contract furniture for bars and restaurants. Again, the rapid growth in the number of stylish venues all over Britain created an urgent need for products, which the Glasgow Collection and its designers were only too happy to help fulfil. The abundance of such projects reflects the fact that we were aiming for every product to become a commercial success, and it was appropriate that we should follow general trends in the market. But there are other objects in the collection which are not so readily categorised. A canal boat project by Zoo Architects established a new way of thinking about the boat as a domestic environment. A rubber neck-guard to protect customers from the uncomfortable experience of finding hairs under the collar at the barber, was the brainchild of Jephson Robb. Whatever the product, all of the ideas supported by the Collection over the past three years have been unquestionably benefited, either financially or otherwise, by their association with the programme.

Changing perceptions

For Hampden Football Stadium, one of the unexpected by-products of this project was that after being involved in the lighting scheme and finding it beneficial and not too painful a process, the stadium's management team began to think about how design could improve other areas, such as graphics on tickets, merchandise and signage. They realised the design process wasn't as threatening to them as they first feared and we had helped to minimise any risks to them. So a new luminaire has helped to change the culture of a football stadium.

The Royal Bank of Scotland has now embraced design through its involvement in the Collection and is prepared to assess design projects requiring financial assistance on their individual merits rather than prescribed criteria, understanding the need to be flexible with creative industries. They are directly supporting twelve projects from the Glasgow Collection, helping each one in a different manner in terms of amount of funding, usage and timescale. This funding complements the support given by the Glasgow Collection. They are keen to continue the relationship, seeking early involvement with start-up companies, and are committed to Glasgow's design community.

The Glasgow Development Agency has been impressed by the economic power of design and has considerably increased its understanding of design and the design process, in particular with the realisation that creativity can be allowed to flourish by being flexible. Equally importantly, the GDA has learnt that we can live with a mix of successes and failures in a design scheme: it is the nature of the process.

Succeeding

Projects have been more likely to succeed where established manufacturers are involved who are being shown new potential markets by design. Involving them in the process of designing rather than presenting them with a finished product that we wanted them to manufacture has ensured they feel more ownership and commitment to the project. UPP's involvement with the Quentin and Uma pulp paper lamps is a good example. UPP's core business is making standard pulp paper components for industrial packaging, but they have just as much investment in the paper lamp products as the designers have, having developed the skills and know how specifically to make them work. Together with the designers they are protecting their joint intellectual property rights.

Timing is crucial to success. Some failures have occurred when producers haven't been ready for product development even though they believed they were. In other cases, designers have been keen to be involved but have not realised both the short and long term commitment necessary to make the product work.

Some other designers didn't fully understand that a great design is not enough: deliverability, cost, sustainable quality and an understanding of the market place are important too. Some couldn't comprehend the scale and totality or how the marketplace develops. Producing a small run is very different from supplying chainstores. Many designers didn't want to be involved in the production and marketing of their product and wanted the Glasgow Collection to handle this though it wasn't our remit. It made a few rethink their commitment to design. If they weren't fully committed we could not risk putting them together with a manufacturer in case it had a very negative impact. Part of the Collection's role has been establishing very creative relationships between manufacturers and designers based on total commitment and, of course, personalities.

Overall, the project has been a resounding success. Since 1997, Glasgow products have been displayed at trade fairs in London and New York, as well as all over Scotland, and they have collected a host of awards along the way. At the International Contemporary Furniture Fair in May 1998, laminates by Timorous Beasties (best known for their fabric and wallpaper designs) were awarded Best Application of Textile Design. Closer to home, the Ursula stainless steel bath was awarded Millennium Products status by the Design Council, and One Foot Taller's Chasm chair won the Best of Show award at the 1998 100% Design exhibition in London. These were the first of no less than 18 awards which have been made to Glasgow Collection products to date [including the Millennium Products]. Most recently, the Chasm chair was awarded the highly prestigious Peugeot Design Award for furniture, at the 1999 100% Design exhibition, Jasper Morrison's Argyll upholstery fabric for Bute Fabrics was awarded the Manufacturers' Award, and a further 6 designs have become Millennium Products. Moreover, Glasgow designers are now being recognised on the international design circuit. One Foot Taller's chair is currently touring Europe in a British Council exhibition devoted to the best of British design, and VK&C's pulped paper light (shortlisted for an award at 100% Design) is widely accepted as offering a genuinely innovative approach to materials in lighting design.

After many years out in the cold, Glasgow is being accepted as an important centre for design. The First Batch exhibition at The Lighthouse in October 1999 offers an opportunity to weigh up the projects in one space for the first time.

Towards the Second Batch

It is a fitting tribute to the designers and manufacturers involved that they have brought the Glasgow design scene into the international limelight, but the process doesn't end there. If the Glasgow Collection is really to prove successful, it will have helped regenerate the spirit of innovation in the city, and will continue to catalyse inventive ideas in the future. If we stop now, the Glasgow Collection will have been an interesting and worthy experiment. By carrying on, we can turn the time, money and energy spent on the project into an investment which will provide a return for the city of Glasgow for many years to come. First Batch, as The Lighthouse exhibition is titled, should be just that; the first of many batches of design projects to be generated in Glasgow. The vital second step must be for the energy and organisational resources which went into the production of the first 51 items in the Glasgow Collection, to be maintained so that the reemergence of the city as a vibrant centre for design excellence can ensure that we generate many, many more.

Bruce Wood is director of the Glasgow Collection.

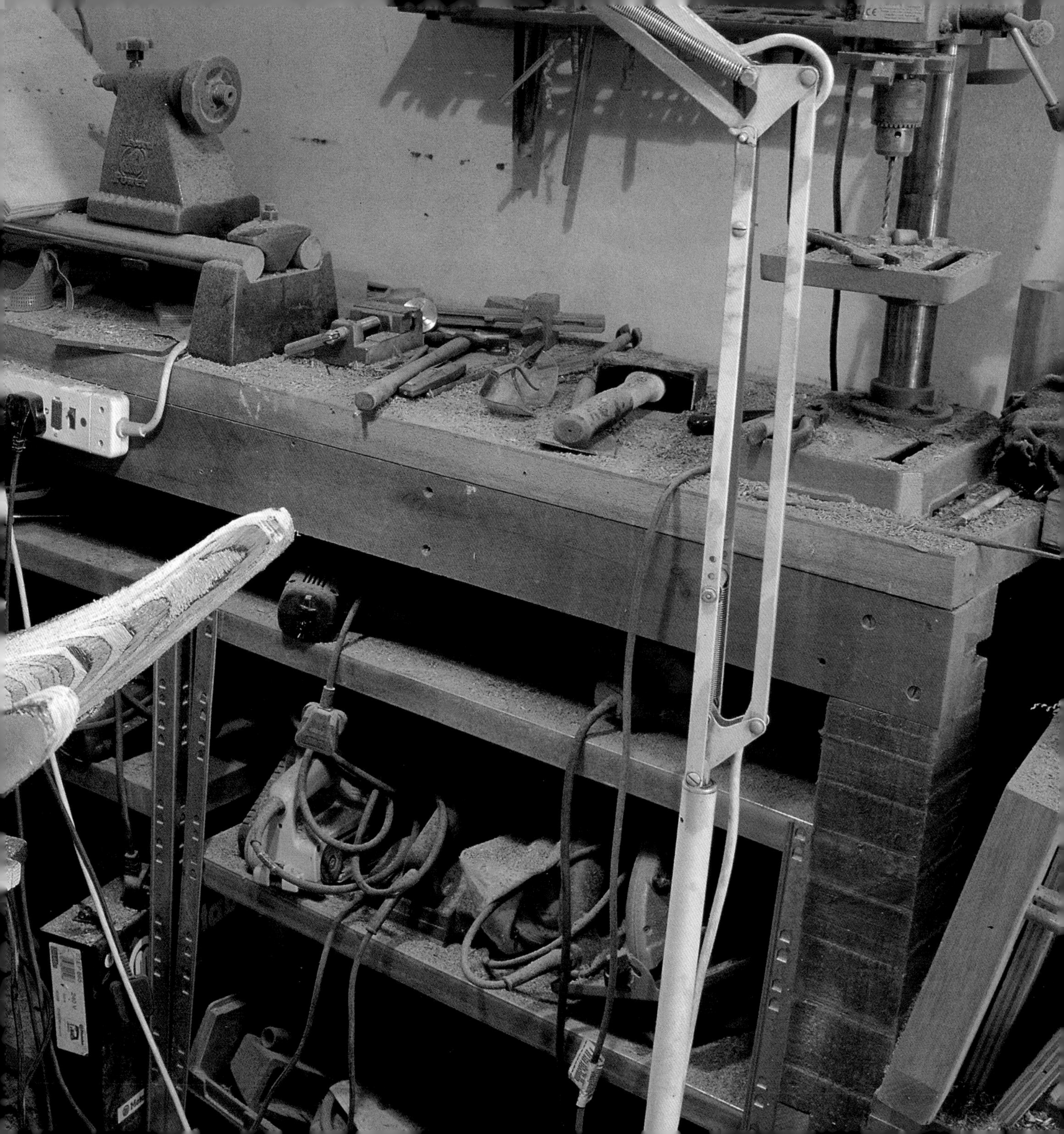

A new kind of brand. The immediate aims of the Collection were refreshingly clear: to promote innovative design in Glasgow, forge new links between the city's manufacturing and design companies and establish the city as an international centre for design. A lack of ambition was never one of the Collection's problems. ***Simon and Sarah Paterson***

Unusually for such a grand design, the Collection was remarkably focused on measurable output. Its target was to identify and develop 60 projects and products that would exemplify the value of co-operation between different parts of the city's economic and creative life. By any standards, as a group, the success of the Collection's products has been outstanding. Seventeen industry and design awards and strong sales prospects indicate the excellence of the output.

It is less easy to judge the success of the Collection in fulfilling its grander aim of establishing Glasgow as an international centre for design. In part this is because the results cannot be said to be in until at least five or even ten years have passed. In addition, the Collection as originally envisaged, realistically could only have been expected to contribute an effective first stage in drawing international attention to Glasgow's cultural, design and manufacturing strengths.

Even so, as part of Glasgow 1999, we think the Collection has attracted enough domestic and international interest to justify a long term commitment by the city. In our role as brand and design management consultants and advisors to the project, the most interesting thing about the Glasgow Collection is not so much that it was a success, but why. If we can identify and understand the factors that made the project work, its success can be sustained in Glasgow and replicated elsewhere.

The Collection was a success because first, it was the right project in the right place at the right time. Second, it developed a powerful, energetic and informal culture early on and that culture was exactly appropriate to the delivery of its explicit short term goals. Third, the Collection had a dynamic, resourceful and well-connected leadership and was organised to minimise bureaucracy. Finally that the project was energised from the start by its short timescale and demanding targets. Some of these factors are clearly situational and though important to understand, are hard to reproduce. Many more relate to management and organisation and these are well worth further exploration.

One of the most striking features of the project was the way in which it very quickly evolved a powerful culture. All of the many people and organisations involved responded to the informal, inventive, fast-moving "can do" attitude which characterised the project's management. These qualities were further reflected in the Collection's organisation, behaviour and, of course, its products. The strength of this culture prevented the Collection from becoming caught up in the kind of dead-handed wranglings and conservativism which so often bedevil demanding multi-disciplinary, multi-interest projects. It had its downside too: ever willing to try out a new idea, this way of doing things also dismissed any idea that didn't work out well quickly. That left the single, sadly unsuccessful, attempt to involve local people in the creative process as a sorry testament to good intentions.

Bureaucracy was kept to the minimum consistent with fairness and accountability. Meetings were (usually) short and purposeful. Ideas and promises were quickly taken up and fulfilled. This was just as well as the Collection's central offer of expert support depended on the goodwill of many busy individuals and organisations. The informality and purpose kept the interest and commitment of all participants and took account of the programme's relative importance to its participants.

Of course, this style was perfect for the short time scale involved. The tension between the demands of very precise public targets and the informal, ad-hoc fluid processes and attitudes worked productively. However, the timescale undoubtedly limited the complexity of the projects the Collection could undertake. If the Collection continues, it may want to retain its drive and sense of urgency by retaining the basic 12 month programme, but run a concurrent 2 year programme to see through a limited number of more complicated projects.

The Collection promised to encourage and develop creative partnerships between finance, design and manufacturing. It delivered. The early establishment of an advisory panel involved talented and experienced individuals and organisations such as the Glasgow Development Agency, the Royal Bank of Scotland, Scottish Design, the industrial designer Sebastian Conran, the design consultant Professor James Woodhuysen (as well as Simon Paterson, the co-author of this essay). They provided important contacts, advice, inspiration and support throughout the project.

The Collection was also, happily, the right project in the right place at the right time. Glasgow was in the process of cultural and economic regeneration and had recognised the importance of design as an economic force. This in itself made it unusual for a city outside mainland Europe. Glasgow had taken stock of its position in the design sector. The city had a thriving but relatively undeveloped and fragmented design industry. It also had a fine but underused resource in the College of Art. Glasgow's manufacturing base was ready to exploit new domestic and international markets. Crucially, the city had good, imaginative relationships between the financial sector and its public administration.

It was, happily, the right project in the right place at the right time

There is no doubt that the experience of the Glasgow Collection offers useful guidelines for the organisation and management of similar projects. It remains to be seen what the future will be for the Collection itself. In the Glasgow Collection, the city has a young brand with the potential to centre and sustain Glasgow's long-term commitment to innovative design and manufacture, and to raise the city's international profile.

The nature of the brand expresses its core values of creative and commercial innovation and invention. It projects the potential of good industrial design and showcases Glasgow's strengths and prospects in this field. It is in some ways a new kind of brand. The Collection is a sort of 'Mother Ship brand', forming short -term project links, nurturing ideas and finally uncoupling as it launches offspring products and alliances. The Collection is a brand that is entirely of the moment: a take something, give something and move on model that is coming to characterise economic relationships and patterns of employment.

The Collection is a sort of 'Mother Ship' brand

Clearly, this kind of relationship brand has something in common with the offers made by universities, art colleges and government development agencies. What is new is the fact that its offer takes the relationship further. The Collection not only gives expertise, contacts, status and impetus; its brand promotes and helps capitalise on successful collaboration.

This is a brand devoted not just to individual personal or corporate success but to the wealth and reputation of a city. It could all too easily fade into the archives of exhibitions past. To thrive, like all brands, the Glasgow Collection will need to be managed. The city and its professional advisers will need to manage the Collection's strategic goals. For the moment, the original grand design to place Glasgow among the world's top centres for industrial design and manufacture seems sufficient to explain its purpose and value. Operational management may present a bigger challenge. A constant flow of fresh ideas and new contacts will be critical to the future success of the Collection.

The stream of inspiration and energy found in the Collection's list of advisors was critical to the success of the whole project. One vital issue for the Collection is how best to maintain the calibre and commitment of the advisory group. There will inevitably be fallow periods, but on the whole we think that the continued success of the brand together with a tradition of realistic expectations should ensure a ready source of professional goodwill and support. With further success, the Collection's selection processes will attract greater interest and scrutiny. Its directors will need to maintain the programme's reputation for fairness and accountability.

This is a brand devoted to the wealth and reputation of a city

As the Collection develops its portfolio, operational goals might focus on particular sectors in industry and take account of the potential of more complex projects requiring longer term commitment. Marketing will obviously be of great importance and the Collection will need to find the expertise and resources to exploit opportunities within the international market. In time, the Collection might well need to find a permanent site in which to display its achievements. The Lighthouse is in an obvious possibility.

The potential of the Glasgow Collection is big enough to take very seriously

As for growth, it is plain that the Collection has so far achieved the right balance between targets and timescale. Any major increase in the number of projects beyond about 25 a year would almost certainly be overwhelming and might well dilute the quality of the Collection's service and output. It would surely tax the existing organisational structure. Growth might best be thought of in terms of international recognition and tangible economic benefit.

The potential of the Glasgow Collection is big enough in commercial and cultural terms to take very seriously. We look forward to its continued success in highlighting Glasgow's proper status as a city where good – and sometimes even great – things happen.

Simon and Sarah Paterson, of the Paterson Brand Consultancy, are brand and design consultants whose experience includes projects with design companies Wolff Olins and Pentagram

Katerina Barac of One Foot Taller with the 'Canyon' armchair

The Collection in detail

The Glasgow Collection consists of 51 projects by 58 designers. It covers household items like lamps, clocks, furniture and tableware as well as sporting equipment, a bath tub and a canal barge. With eighteen of the items developed as part of Collection already in production, the targets set for this first phase of the project have been exceeded.

Chasm
Chair

Ravine
Dining chair

Bone china lamp

One Foot Taller

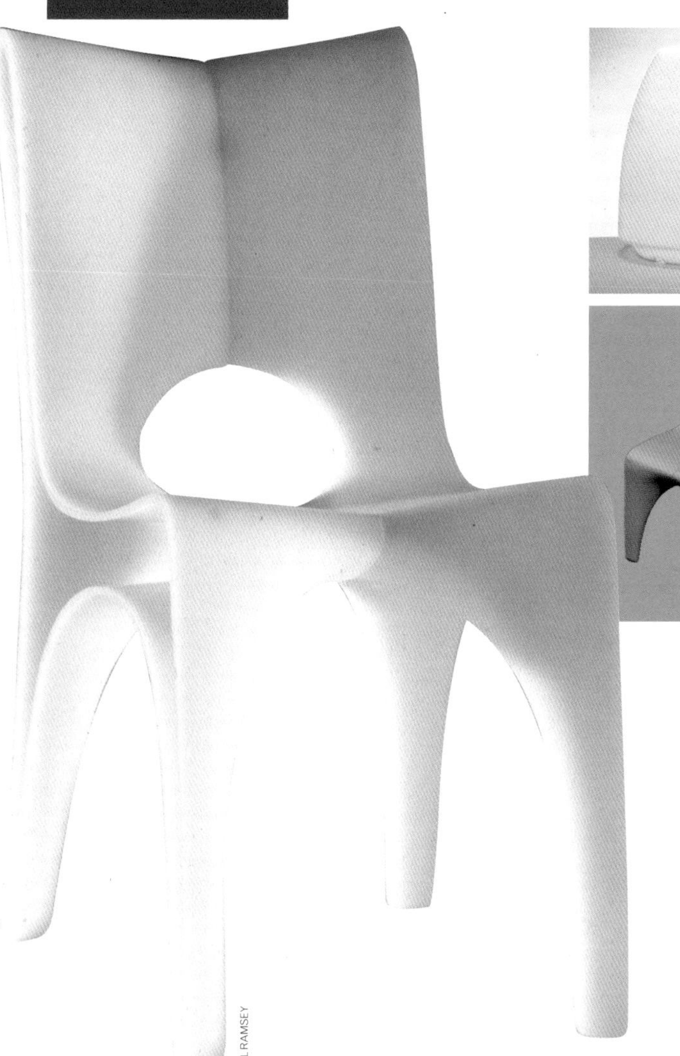

NEIL RAMSEY

PICTURES ON THE WALL

PICTURES ON THE WALL

Above: Bone china lamp, *Ravine* dining chair
Left: *Chasm* chair

The *Chasm* chair has won designers One Foot Taller many new friends and almost as many awards. It was named Best of Show on its launch at *100% Design* in London in 1998, received Millennium Product status and netted Will White and Katarina Barac the inaugural Peugeot Design Award (worth £15,000) in May 1999. Its success has moved One Foot Taller's work into the international spotlight and onto a different level.

Chasm was designed for Glasgow retailer Nice House, whose proprietor, Andy Harrold, encouraged the Glasgow School of Art graduates to think about the possibilities of mass production for the first time. The design process was made possible by support from the Glasgow Collection.

The chair is manufactured by Plastic Dip Mouldings in Irvine, a company which usually uses the same technique and equipment to produce traffic cones. The costs for tooling and set-up of rotational moulding are a fraction of those for the more sophisticated injection moulding, but White and Barac's design solution turned the limitations of their chosen method of production (and their budget) to their advantage. The basic moulded form that comes off the production line looking like a rather odd two-legged chair is sawn in half down the middle, and the two sections are bolted together "inside out", showing off *Chasm*'s hollow core.

For One Foot Taller, the success of *Chasm* means no longer having to work on the kitchen table of Will White's cramped flat, surrounded by hand-produced objects. White and Barac have gone on to make use of a grant from the Royal Bank of Scotland to develop *Ravine,* a taller, higher backed version suitable for use as a dining chair, while a laid-back armchair version (made for Glasgow 1999's *Homes for the Future* project) has also been developed. The *Pup* furniture range, their collaboration with textile designers Timourous Beasties, can be seen in Strata, yet another of Glasgow's ever-increasing number of stylish drinking dens, along with the fine bone china lamp made possible by further Royal Bank of Scotland support and the input of ceramics specialists Fireworks.

Solo
Flat pack clock

P.o.D.S
Display units

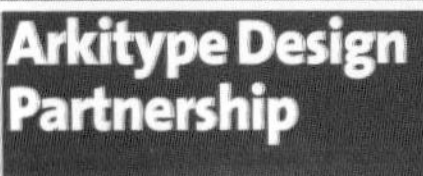

Arkitype Design Partnership

ALAISDAIR SMITH

Not long after graduating from Glasgow School of Art's product design course in 1996, Richard Smith, Douglas Bryden and Stephen Young formed the Arkitype Design Partnership. The team soon discovered that when it came to designing and manufacturing furniture, it was impossible to compete with larger manufacturers, and decided to concentrate on smaller, more cost-effective products instead.

The *Solo* clock, made out of a single sheet of thin, flexible but strong polypropylene, was based on the young designers' experiments with sheets of paper. The colourful clock comes flat-packed and ready to assemble, making it easy for retailers to store and an ideal gift to send through the post. "The Glasgow Collection stepped in just before we went into production," says Stephen Young. "The money we were given eased a lot of the pressure involved in independently launching a new product to the market." The worldwide success of the *Solo* clock and other flat-pack polypropylene products has inspired Arkitype to expand the range to include a picture frame, a waste paper basket and a flat-pack vase they promise is watertight.

Linking up with the Glasgow Collection also led to an invitation from Bruce Wood and Stuart MacDonald, the Director of *The Lighthouse*, to design mobile exhibition units for the Glasgow Open Museum. These units were to house an exhibition of product design, put together to raise public awareness of both the opening of *The Lighthouse* and design in general.

"The units we designed consisted of a series of flight cases which could be wheeled around and lifted easily by two people," says Young. The *P.o.D.S.* display units, which come complete with their own lighting system, are two-tiered: an opening at the front of the case serving as a plinth allows viewers to handle some of the exhibits, while the sealed upper display level is used for delicate or valuable items. No space is wasted: during transit, the Perspex cases are protected by upholstered vinyl panels, which later fold down over the sides of the flight cases to create, in the words of Young, a "tactile alternative to the standard plinth".

Pup Laminated furniture

Timorous Beasties, One Foot Taller

When design duo Timorous Beasties decided to diversify and apply their textile designs to furniture, they might easily have stuck to upholstery and loose covers. But instead of settling for soft furnishings, Paul Simmons and Alistair McAuley teamed up with the Glasgow Collection and made their designs available in a completely different format – as sub-surface wood laminates.

In Simmons and McAuley's hands, a material more commonly used for corporate logos, plain-coloured panels and in-store signage is given a new lease of life. The designers persuaded manufacturers Novograf to take the unusual step of producing some laminates with a clear backing, which allows the grain of the wood to which it is applied show through. This gives added depth and interest to a range of designs and patterns made up of targets, spiralling arrows and eye-popping op-art graphics.

Apart from winning the award for best laminates at the *International Contemporary Furniture Fair* in New York, the range also achieved Millennium Product status in 1999.

In the light of these successes, Timorous Beasties collaborated with designers One Foot Taller to develop a range of furniture using the laminates. The resulting *Pup* range, manufactured by Morris of Glasgow, includes a high-backed dining chair, a simple U-shaped stool, a table and a bar stool. The furniture was specified in Strata, a bar on Glasgow's Queen Street which also boasts a wall covered entirely in a Timorous Beasties laminate.

For Simmons and McAuley, this is only the beginning. They believe their laminates have great potential in all kinds of environments. A whole airport covered in their signature style, for example? Don't put it past them.

NEIL RAMSEY

Glasgow 1999 Outdoor Luminaire

Philips Lighting Ltd

NEIL RAMSEY

Unless you are a keen amateur star gazer with a love of dark night skies, the threat of light pollution may not be the first thing that comes to mind when considering the potential drawbacks of living next door to a 52,000-capacity football and rugby stadium. But for Scotland's new National Stadium, located in the middle of a built-up residential area, avoiding excessively bright lighting was an issue that needed careful consideration.

The recent revamp of Hampden Stadium provided an opportunity to take a fresh look at the site's lighting. Basic towering floodlights would have been inappropriate here, so the Glasgow Collection team proposed a project to help the stadium's management team select a new type of light to suit its specific needs. Three very different companies were invited to present concept ideas for a lighting system designed to human scale: design consultancy Graven Images, architectural practice McKeown Alexander and experienced industrial designer Gerald Taylor. This project provided a very effective lesson in the art of the collaborative design process: all three conceptual designs, made possible by the support of the Glasgow Collection, were in turn passed on to Philips Lighting. The company, which has production facilities in the area, then came up with its own proposal and was responsible for the final design and the manufacture of the light.

The *Glasgow 1999 Outdoor Luminaire*, as it is officially known, is already in place on the south side of Hampden stadium and has also been taken up as part of the Philips International Lighting range. The luminaire combines two functions: the lower of its columns carries the lamp, complete with a reflector bowl, while the taller second column serves as a flagpole. The luminaire does everything required of a light in this situation: it looks elegant, it is strong enough to stand up to the crowds and the indirect lighting system ensures that the entire neighbourhood isn't lit up like a Christmas tree when a night-time match is being played.

Quentin Uma Paper pulp lamps

VK&C Partnership

Egg cartons might not be the most obvious source of design inspiration, but with their *Quentin* and *Uma* lampshades the VK&C Partnership have proved that there can be more to moulded paper pulp than you might have thought. "It has taken many experiments to obtain a repeatable recipe for the pulp which produces the translucency we were after," says Hamid van Koten of the VK&C Partnership. "But it looks like we have finally cracked it and in conjunction with the manufacturer, we are now considering patenting the recipe."

Made of recycled paper mill waste, both lamps were designed specifically for use with energy-saving compact fluorescent bulbs. When lit, the semi-translucent rough-textured pulp provides a surprisingly subtle glow. The *Quentin* pendant lamp won the award for Best Use of Paper in the Scottish Design Awards, and was also named Best Consumer Product at the *Design Week* Awards in 1999. VK&C have equally high hopes for newly-launched sister product *Uma*, made using the same techniques. *Uma*

Bop
Table lamp

ALAISDAR SMITH

GUS MILL

Left: ***Uma***
Far left: ***Quentin***
Below: ***Bop***

consists of a single folded paper moulding, held together with poppers, and with the right accessories it can be used as a table lamp, a floor lamp or a wall light. The product was made possible by a grant from the Royal Bank of Scotland, who understood the importance for the company of getting another product on to the market quickly. The Glasgow Collection was involved from the earliest stages of the project. "They gave us a lot of support with the tooling which we would never have been able to fund ourselves," says van Koten.

The starting point of VK&C's relationship with the Collection was the *Bop* lamp, which the designers had developed to a rough prototype stage before receiving the funding they needed for an initial production run of 100 lamps. *Bop* is a low voltage table lamp with an adjustable nylon "sail" that is stretched between curved stainless steel rods anchored in a cast concrete base. VK&C have sold small batches of *Bops* to retail outlets, as well as directly to the public by mail order, but believe that the pulp lamps, with their lower production costs, will prove to be the more accessible products.

Ideally, Hamid van Koten would like to see the Glasgow Collection follow the example of European initiatives like the Droog Collection, which has a separate arm dedicated to producing, marketing and selling all Droog products. "For small design companies like us, dealing with the sale of our products is difficult – we were never trained to do this, and to be honest we don't really want to. If the Glasgow Collection takes this on board, then it can truly change things both for local designers and industry, and eventually make a difference to the Scottish economy."

NEIL RAMSEY

Skins
Digital hand drum

Ben Smith, Digital Cow with David Bernard, Sound Surgery

Designer and percussionist Ben Smith is making a noise in the music industry. A recent Product Design graduate of the Glasgow School of Art, Smith has developed his final year project by designing a radically new musical interface in the form of an electronic hand-drum.

Skins combines an array of pressure sensitive pads, squeezable rubber extensions and a multitude of sequencing buttons to create a much more hands-on playing experience than other conventional drum machines. Designed in collaboration with David Bernard from Sound Surgery, who provided electronics expertise, the drum stores sounds and beats, ready to use and manipulate in a live performance or in the studio. A thumb-operated wheel allows for changes in parameters can alter sounds and change tones on various parts of the drum. Smith's design balances ergonomics with animated colours, making for an object that will not only bring the house down, but will look good too, thereby producing a design which is seen as an instrument to be played, rather than just a programmable machine.

Smith and Bernard, collectively known as Dubweiser, have already wowed audiences with *Skins* performances – not least the Glasgow Collection board members, who were invited by director Bruce Wood to a special preview to bring them up to speed with the project's progress. With funding from the Glasgow Collection, Smith was able to set up his own company, called Digital Cow, through which he hopes to manufacture and distribute the drums, which have achieved Millennium Product status.

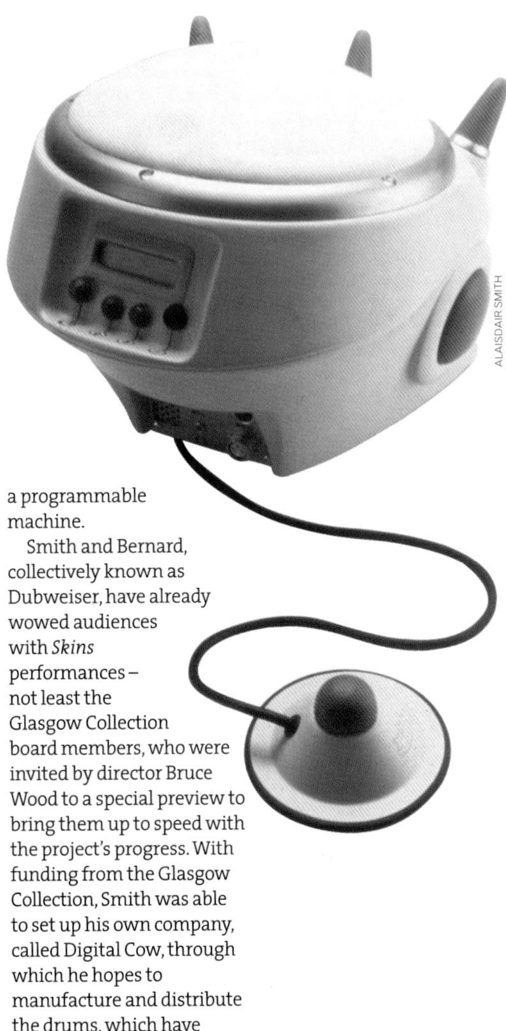

ALAISDAIR SMITH

Leather bags

Frank Gallacher

Frank Gallacher only started making bags because accessories seemed a more manageable proposition for a new fashion business than clothes. That didn't quite turn out to be the case, but for Gallacher, a trained fashion designer who had previously worked for Nicole Farhi, the experience was invaluable.

Early funding from the Glasgow Collection enabled Gallacher to buy the equipment he needed to produce high quality samples. Over the next 18 months, he produced two small collections of structured, architectural bags which he sold to shops around Glasgow and in London. They were very well received, even if the positive response was never quite matched by sales. Gallacher takes a realistic view of the luxury end of the accessories market: "When it's a matter of parting with their hard-earned cash, people go for the established names like Prada, even though my bags are much more interesting..."

Having dealt with the technical difficulties and manufacturing problems of producing high quality leather goods, Gallacher is now looking forward to returning to the relative freedom of designing garments. As the only fashion-based business to receive support from the Glasgow Collection, Gallacher intends to move on and apply all he has learnt to his next steps: "It's a matter of being able to plot out a course of action and stick to it. I still have the same things that inspire me, but I don't feel that I have to continue making the bags for now."

Contemporary ceramics

Yam Design

One of the first projects to receive support from the Glasgow Collection was a range of ceramics designed by Yen Mo and Alan McKeown, who graduated from Glasgow School of Art in 1997. The designers, who were working together as Yam Design at the time, originally developed the project for Drumchapel Opportunities, an agency set up to retrain the long-term unemployed in Glasgow. As some participants in the Drumchapel scheme had expressed an interest in working with ceramics, Yam Designs set out to produce a collection of slipcast ceramics in clear contemporary shapes and colours that the retraining group would be able to manufacture. The final collection, which included an egg pillow, a single stem vase, a nobbly presentation plate and an ashtray, was very well received, however Drumchapel Opportunities have not been able to progress the project any further so far.

NEIL RAMSEY

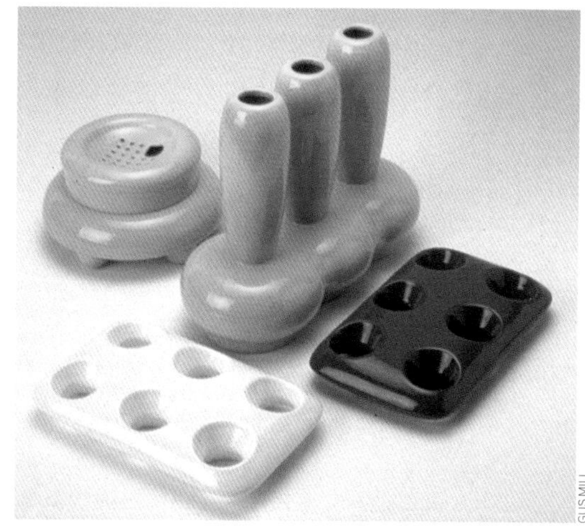

GUS MILL

Recycled plastic outdoor furniture

VK&C Partnership
Paul Pearson
Jules Goss

Below left: Sineseat, by VK&C
Left: design sketches by Jules Goss
Below: solid bench by Paul Pearson

NEIL RAMSEY

Making the right connections is an important element of the Glasgow Collection, but sometimes perfect combinations do present themselves by chance. A company approached as a possible supporter of Glasgow 1999 had a potentially interesting but as yet under-utilised material made from waste plastic to offer as sponsorship in kind. Around the same time, the city's Parks Department approached the Collection about the possibility of finding new designs for outdoor furniture. It turned out that Plaswood, the recycled plastic material supplied by Dumfries Polythene Recycling, would lend itself perfectly for outdoor use: it is heavy, no more vulnerable to damage from fire than wood and its paint-resistant nature makes it virtually vandal-proof. A new Glasgow Collection project was born.

Three very different designers were selected by the Glasgow Collection for the project: one of them, Paul Pearson, was fresh out of college (he graduated from Glasgow School of Art in 1998), while up-and-coming Glasgow-based designers VK&C are Glasgow Collection veterans – their *Bop*, *Quentin* and *Uma* lamps were made possible by Glasgow 1999 funding. The third designer, Jules Goss, came at the project from a more unusual angle, being a sculptor by profession. Each designer took one or two pieces through to prototype stage to present to Glasgow's Parks Department. The designers were not asked to design their piece for a specific place, but the very diverse characters of the resulting furniture once again reinforce the importance of making the perfect match, in this case

between product and location.

VK&Cs curved *Sineseat*, for example, would work well with the elegant domed greenhouses of Glasgow's Botanic Gardens. The designers made good use of Plaswood's inherent flexibility bendiness by developing a seating system that designed to curve around specific site features. The system is, in theory, endlessly extendable, with the seating slats anchored by cast aluminium supports with optional backs.

Paul Pearson's solid bench could easily be imagined in a more urban setting, or down by the banks of the Clyde. The young designer chose to combine the Plaswood seating elements with heavy concrete supports, concealing the fixing mechanisms with brushed steel details. This modular system is already being producted for specific clients, most recently the Glasgow Orientation Centre.

The sculptural pieces designed by Jules Goss would suit a gallery environment. He bolted together individual planks of Plaswood to form a heavy, monolithic slab, which is supported by refined cast-aluminium legs.

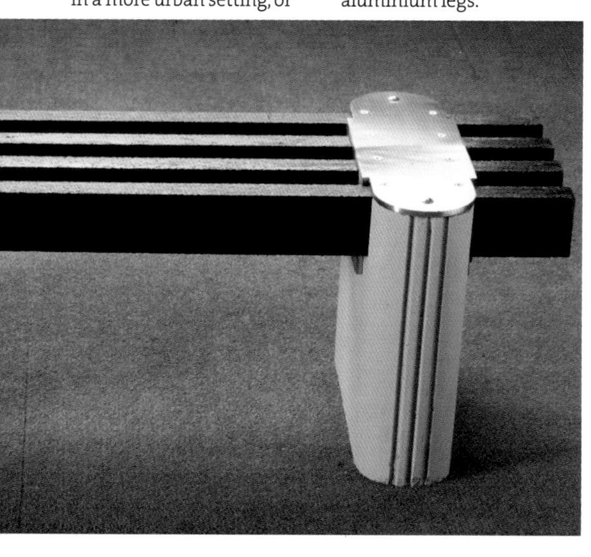

Vortex Dinghy Sail

Adrian Shields

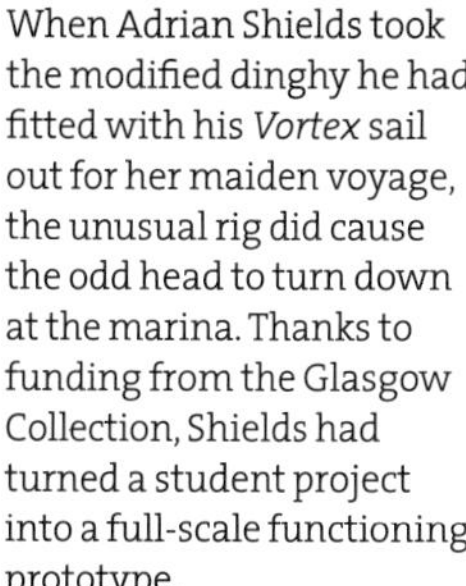

When Adrian Shields took the modified dinghy he had fitted with his *Vortex* sail out for her maiden voyage, the unusual rig did cause the odd head to turn down at the marina. Thanks to funding from the Glasgow Collection, Shields had turned a student project into a full-scale functioning prototype.

While the finished sail might not look quite as sleek as Shields originally hoped it would (high tooling costs made it impossible to have all the parts custom made), it has proved to be very effective in practise. The design is based on the crab claw shape common to traditional Polynesian boats, with the crucial difference that Shields' version allows the mast to rotate, thereby making tacking much easier and the boat more efficient and manoeuvrable.

Adrian Shields, who graduated from Glasgow School of Art's Product Design Engineering department in 1998, describes the process of producing the prototype as "a nightmare, but enjoyable". He finished it in his spare time, when he wasn't working at his day job as a designer for companies including

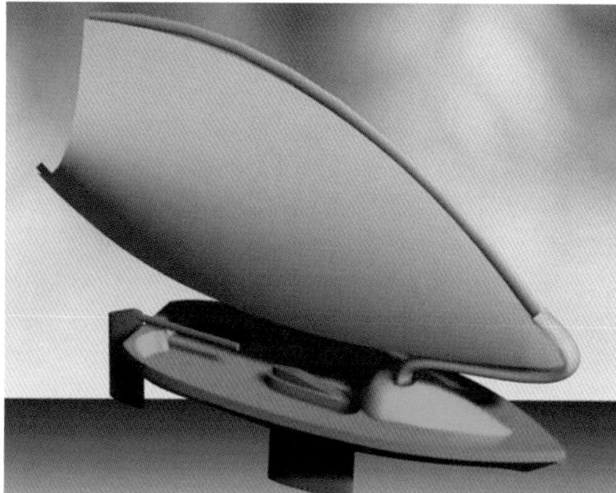

Glasgow firm Wallace Cameron (which is also represented in the Glasgow Collection with its *First Aid Dispensers*, page 45). Shields found the experience of making his first full-scale product very useful: "I've made some really good new contacts doing this, and the experience has enabled me to see how I could to do other things in the future."

The team which built Ursula. Designers Jon Barnes and Nicola Regan flanked by John Clarke and Philip Tolan (right) of Associated Metal

Case study
Associated Metal and the Ursula bath tub
Philip Tolan

Philip Tolan, who runs the stainless steel manufacturing company Associated Metal, first learnt about the *Ursula* project when designer Jon Barnes of Submarine contacted him. "He had seen our permanent product display at the Building Centre in London," says Tolan. "And when he discovered that we were a Glasgow-based company, he approached us immediately." Barnes was interested in realising his idea of a bath in stainless steel, and had recently received funding to develop the project from the Glasgow Collection.

"We had quite a number of meetings with Submarine, first of all to look at the bath in its concept form, and then throughout the development of the product. It was vital that we collaborated closely." says Tolan. "We were already known to certain people within the GDA, but Bruce Wood had not visited us before, so we were delighted when he came along." It was the beginning of a collaboration which may well benefit Associated Metals in a number of ways, as the *Ursula* bath itself has made a powerful impact on the luxury end of the market, and a range of other *Ursula* bathroom products are now planned.

For Tolan, the company's experience in manufacturing helped to make *Ursula* a better product: "We have been around since 1907, and we began working with stainless steel as soon as it first became available in the 1930s. By the 1950s we had begun making stainless steel sanitary ware – WC pans, urinals and so on, mainly for commercial applications such as hospitals and prisons. But from time to time we also make stainless steel bathroom suites for individuals too. So when Jon Barnes approached us we knew we had enough experience to be able to help. Equally importantly, as a company we have a hand-crafting capacity as well as laser cutting machines. For Ursula every stage requires an exceptional number of man-hours: from sheet metal assembly; welding; grinding down the welds; blending the welds into the sheet material; right through to polishing the entire surface."

The in house team at Associated Metal worked closely with the designers to come up with a formula that would work. "The design for the bath was by Submarine, but it was necessary to bring our experience to bear in order to ensure that the product could be made. Having said that, we work with architects and designers regularly and it is important to maintain the essence of what people are looking for, while bringing that together with a manufacturing technique which will be cost effective. Submarine came in with sketches and a template for Ursula: our input was quite significant, and we are delighted with the result.

Although this is not the first design-led project that Associated Metal have worked on ("We have also developed a floor-to-ceiling urinal called *Euro Waterfall* for a number of night clubs in Britain."), Tolan is convinced that the Glasgow Collection will have a far-reaching effect, and will lead to further design innovation, not least at Associated Metal itself. "The high profile of the exercise is bound to bring more possibilities to Glasgow as a manufacturing base and like other people, we expect to benefit. It really does seem to have opened people's eyes, not only in the Scottish market but in Europe as a whole."

Philip Tolan is Managing Director of Associated Metal (Stainless) Ltd

Ursula Stainless steel bath

Submarine

JON BARNES

Every new furniture design company is faced with the problem of deciding what to make first. A table? A chair? An ideal first product gets people's attention, even without the aid of a big advertising budget. With the *Ursula* bathtub, Submarine have certainly achieved that goal. The first product to be selected for Glasgow Collection support, *Ursula* was launched at *100% Design* in London in 1997, and has since won the Editors Award for Craftsmanship at *ICFF* in New York as well as a Smart Award from the Glasgow Development Agency. It has been selected by Sir Terence Conran for inclusion in an exhibition of the best of recent British design at the Philadelphia Museum of Art in the United States and has achieved Millennium Product status.

In many ways, a bathtub was an ideal place to start: not only is it a simple shape without any moving parts, made in one place from one material, but it is also a relatively unexplored product in design terms. On the other hand, no-one could be sure there was a market for huge, custom-made stainless steel baths. "We took a calculated risk when we chose *Ursula* as our first product," says Jon Barnes, who founded Submarine with partner Nicky Regan. "Our philosophy was that we would start at the top, with the most difficult and expensive product, and then work backwards."

Submarine originally set out with the aim of designing beautiful pieces of furniture, not just for the bathroom. But the success of *Ursula* has led to the development of other products in a similar vein: you can have the complete *Ursula* suite. The bath, which was on display at the Boffi stand at the Milan Furniture Fair in 1999, can now be purchased from upmarket retailers CP Hart.

Jon Barnes describes the tub as the Aston Martin of the bathroom, hand-built by skilled craftsmen. Even if Submarine could find someone willing to put up the large sum of money needed to machine-produce *Ursula*, it wouldn't be the same. And because each tub is made to order, the size and shape can be adjusted to suit different requirements and difficult spaces. Finding a manufacturer wasn't easy, but Barnes is full of praise for Associated Metal, the Glasgow firm which makes *Ursula*. "The quality of everything they make is exemplary," says Barnes of the family firm more used to producing stainless steel prison issue toilets than luxury bathtubs. "But I think they're still always surprised by our obsession with elegance and beauty."

First aid and eye wash dispenser

Wallace Cameron

It's almost 50 years since the Wallace Cameron Group started manufacturing first aid kits. In that time, the basic design of a piece of equipment found as a standard requirement in offices, factories and cars everywhere has hardly changed. In March 1998, the company presented the results of extensive research and design development work, supported by the Glasgow Collection, which was spent on rethinking Wallace Cameron's key products.

A leap forward from the familiar flimsy green case, the new Wallace Cameron First Aid Kit is smart, strong, hygienic and above all easy to use. A key feature for every first aid product has to be accessibility, so this case can either be wall mounted, used free-standing or carried to the scene of an accident. Its attractive styling should also help it avoid the all too common fate of being hidden away in the back of the office cupboard. The lid opens up at the touch of a button, revealing a neat interior where each product fits into its own separate compartment. The dispenser, which is manufactured in Scotland from tough, durable ABS plastic, comes complete with an accident report book and an easy to follow guide to first aid. Both the first aid kit and its sister product, an eye wash dispenser, have achieved Millennium Product status.

But the most innovative feature can be found on the kit's outer casing, where a flap pulls down to open a separate plaster dispenser. Thanks to a clever dispensing mechanism, each plaster is delivered with part of the adhesive strip already exposed, making it easier to tend to those small cuts and injuries using just one hand. Addressing and solving everyday problems like that is exactly what you would expect from a company with a chairman whose other projects include developing a cling film dispenser that actually works.

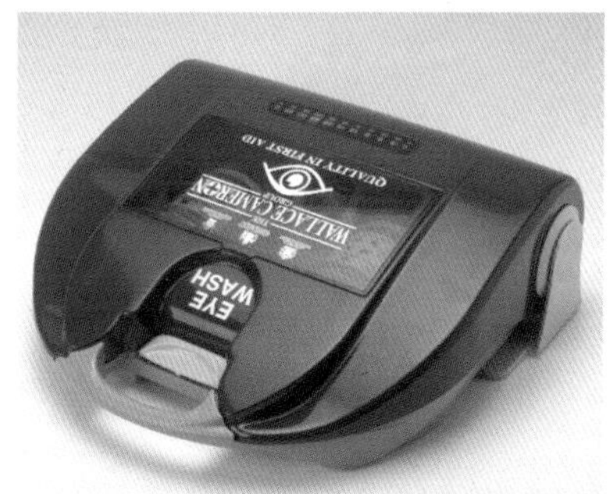

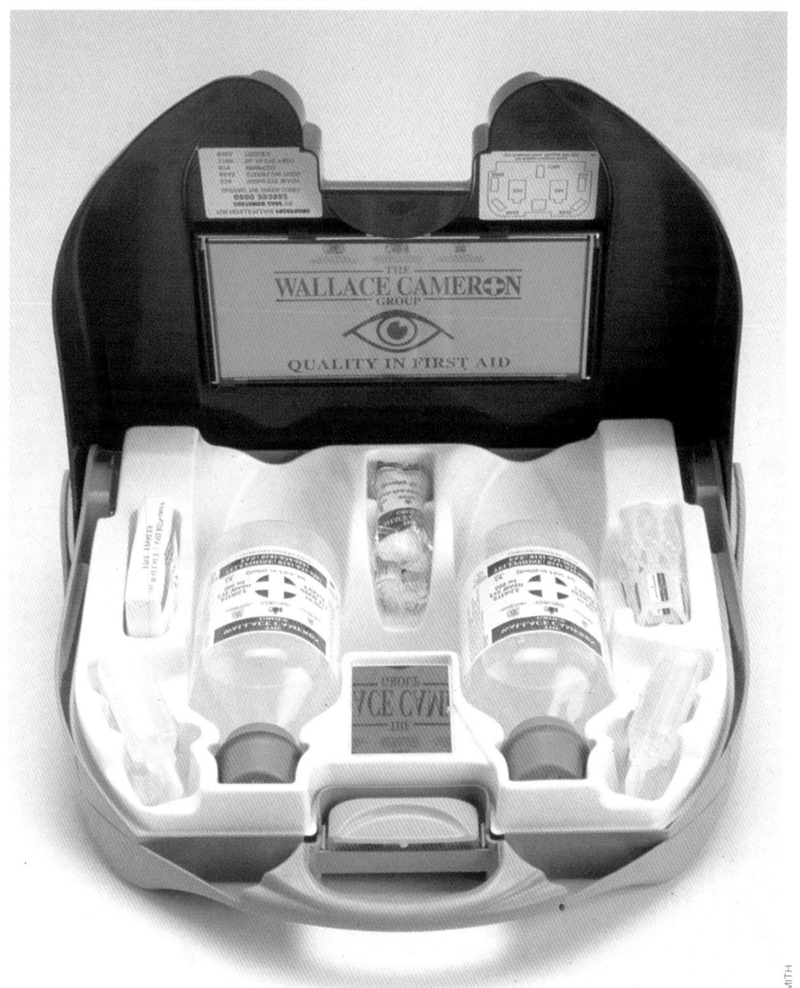

ALAISDAIR SMITH

Hidden 'til lit
Design concepts

McGavigans

McGavigans specialises in developing the technology that makes the instruments on car dashboards light up and the glowing display panels on mobile telephones and video recorders come to life. Realising that this technology had been pushed as far as it would go in mature markets, the well-established Glasgow company decided it was time to consider the possibility of diversification.

McGavigans approached Bruce Wood, who suggested looking at the company's work from a designer's point of view. A concept design project was set up with the support of Scottish Design and design companies were asked to consider other applications for McGavigans' technology and the design possibilities it offered. The four firms that accepted the challenge were established London-based brand specialists Fitch, Primal Design in Glasgow, Crombie Anderson Associates in Dunfermline and Factory Design, a young team of product designers in London responsible for the design of the *Sonus* amplifier in the Glasgow Collection.

The involvement of the Glasgow Collection extended to the support of this 2D conceptual phase, the results of which were taken up by McGavigans and analysed for their marketing and manufacturing feasibility.

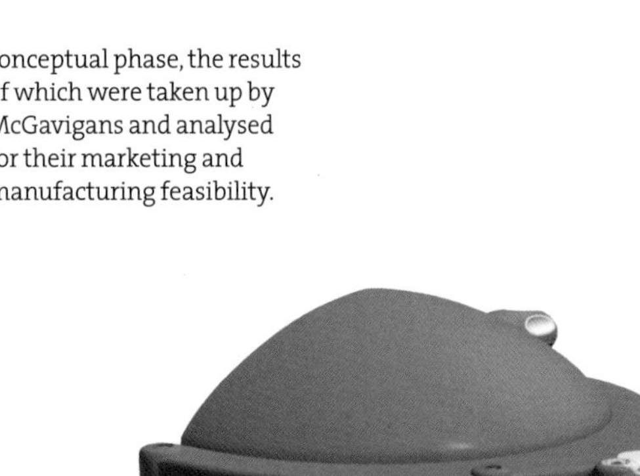

Dante
Portable gas heater

Kirsten Hough

PICTURES ON THE WALL

Canister gas is the Cinderella of the heating industry: it may be a cheap and portable way to heat a room, but the look of this type of gas heater has hardly changed in 25 years. Kirsten Hough, a recent graduate of Glasgow School of Art's product design course, felt the time was right for a new product that "readdresses the market, and diversifies its image away from its firmly planted roots as a boring grey box." Rather than trying to hide the nature of the product by going for the full fake fireplace effect, Hough set out to be contemporary and honest. It turned out to be an approach with practical benefits. "Basing the design around the shape of the gas canister itself has allowed the unit to be very compact", says Hough. "This also aids transparency, storage and causes minimal disruption when the heater is *in situ*."

While Hough set out to prove that it was possible to design an efficient and affordable heater that also looked good, it was vital that this particular cute household item on wheels (which bears a passing resemblance to R2-D2) also conformed to the gas industry's stringent health and safety laws. The young designer worked closely with the industry and suppliers on the development of *Dante*, whose body is formed by two sections of extruded aluminium that function as the main heat radiator. The large surface area and good air circulation allow for efficient heat transfer through both radiation and convection. The design is both economical to produce and easy to use – the gas canister can be accessed and changed without difficulty.

Additional support from the Royal Bank of Scotland will allow Hough to produce a fully-functioning prototype that is ready for safety testing. If taken up by the gas heater industry, *Dante* could retail for around £80, helping to make freezing workshops, studios and sub-zero student accommodation a thing of the past.

Spring, Scooby and Lolli
Children's furniture

Craig Whittet

Left: Spring
Below left: Lolli chair
Below: Scooby

Craig Whittet believes that working with the Glasgow Collection has provided great opportunities for the city's young designers: "You could look at this experience as a different approach to post-graduate design education – getting funding to go out and actually try to get something made."

The product designer, who completed his MA at Glasgow School of Art in 1996, developed three items of children's furniture – the *Scooby* storage system, the *Lolli* chair and the soft *Spring* play mat. First he identified and approached a potential client – the local council, which was planning to open two new playcentres. Then he worked closely with playcentre staff to design furniture that suited the requirements of the adults, appealed to the children and was within the council's budget. According to Whittet, working with clients used to selecting furniture from the pages of a catalogue brought its own problems: "I think they sometimes wished I was telepathic."

While the financial support from the Collection helped make potential manufacturers take him more seriously, getting prototypes made was not easy. In order to avoid the seams and sagging common to upholstered covers, he chose to finish the flexible foam pieces of *Lolli* and *Spring* with a PVC spray coating sometimes used for medical products. Because this technique had not been used for children's furniture before, the pieces proved much more difficult to finish to the necessary standards than he had expected. The only step Whittet needs to complete now is the final and most important one: getting an order and going into production.

CRAIG WHITTET

Haiku, Exo and Porcini
Ceramic tableware

Fireworks

Below: Exo vessel, Porcini tableware

"The best domestic products make everyday tasks more enjoyable," says Tom Elliott of Fireworks. "I want to design things that make people appreciate what they're doing. I'm trying to undermine frenetic modern lifestyles, in a small way."

With help from the Glasgow Collection, Fireworks has made the leap from producing hand made one-offs to working as designers with industry. Elliott and his partner Jackie Alexander have put a range of tableware into production as well as two elegant fruit plates – the glass *Haiku* dish and the ceramic *Exo* Vessel. Their *Porcini* tableware, which was shortlisted for the Peugeot Design Award in 1999, is already being shipped around the world, using specially commissioned packaging made possible by a grant from the Royal Bank of Scotland, negotiated with help of the Glasgow Collection.

The *Porcini* range consists of six simple, multi-functional pieces, which people are encouraged to use in different ways and combinations. The espresso cup and saucer can be turned upside down and used as an egg cup and egg warmer. The cappuccino cup and its saucer double up as a dip bowl or serving vessel, while the larger shallow dish is ideal for rice and pasta.

Elliott is already working on a commercial version of *Porcini*, designed to be suitable for hotels or coffee shops. He sees scope for development in all their products – the *Haiku* plate, for example, could make a wonderful wall light. "Without the Glasgow Collection, we'd still be at square two, instead of heading towards the finish line with smiles on our faces. But that support is worth nothing if we don't take things further ourselves now."

ALAISDAIR SMITH

Concept canal barge

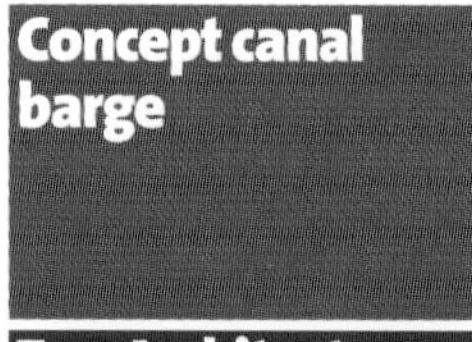

Zoo Architects

ZOO ARCHITECTS

If Zoo Architects have their way, living on the water will no longer mean putting up with the cramped cabins and polished brass of a converted narrow boat or settling for a permanently moored floating pre-fab. A re-working of the traditional canal barge by the Glasgow-based practice combines all the comfort and style you would expect from a contemporary, architect-designed home with the freedom of living wherever you choose.

Designed for use on both canals and coastal waters, the boat is wider than an average barge, giving it enough stability to sail on open water and withstand conditions up to a Force 6 gale. This makes crossing the channel in a houseboat a real possibility, giving access to a remarkable network of navigable canals that stretches across Europe all the way to China. The extra space also allows for more generous, open living spaces than those usually found on narrow boats.

The architects developed the boat for clients Nick Millar and Minty McDonald. The 10-year veterans of houseboat living had already commissioned naval architect Charles Gifford to undertake an outline study for a new type of houseboat when they met Zoo Architects, who took on the design of the living accommodation in the boat using a vocabulary normally associated with land-based housing. At a very early stage, Zoo approached the Glasgow Collection for support with research and design development of the habitable spaces. "Without the Glasgow Collection, the boat project would have stayed at the periphery of our core activities," says Peter Richardson of Zoo Architects. "Their support gave the project focus and exposure to other agencies." The result of this phase of the project was a 1:10 scale model and a set of detailed design drawings. Now, Zoo are keen to find the funds for a working prototype so that Richardson's vision of the future can come true: "It's simple: The boat is built, the ship sails and we get global orders."

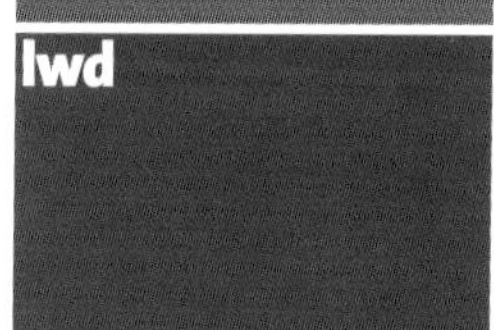

Sam Booth of lwd is very pleased with the way his display system for *The Lighthouse* turned out, describing the finished system as being like "big Lego" – a series of building blocks that can form different configurations by using the individual elements in a multitude of ways. "You can use them upside down, inside out, create lit pockets, repaint the panels, build walls, floors – do anything." So all you need to create whole new spaces within the building's existing galleries is a screwdriver, an allen key and a little imagination.

When Glasgow-based design company lwd won the contract to design the interiors of *The Lighthouse* with Javier Mariscal, part of the job involved developing a display system for the building. "We thought that the best approach would be to devise a flexible exhibition system that could be formatted in different ways with minimum cost for every show," says Sam Booth. "So ideally, each exhibition wouldn't have to be built from scratch." Four basic aluminium frames can be combined and linked using connecting elements to build walls, complex structures or just simple plinths. The framework is then clad with U-shaped plywood panels and clear acrylic bubbles that simply click into place.

Funding from the Glasgow Collection allowed lwd to go ahead with the prototyping of their as yet completely untried idea, which changed quite considerably during the development process. "The Glasgow Collection lets you start off with one idea, but then allows you to evolve them further," says Booth. "We had the freedom to take risks, and try things in a variety of different ways."

NEIL RAMSEY

Yo-Yo
Height adjustable table

Michael Kavanagh
Zebra Design

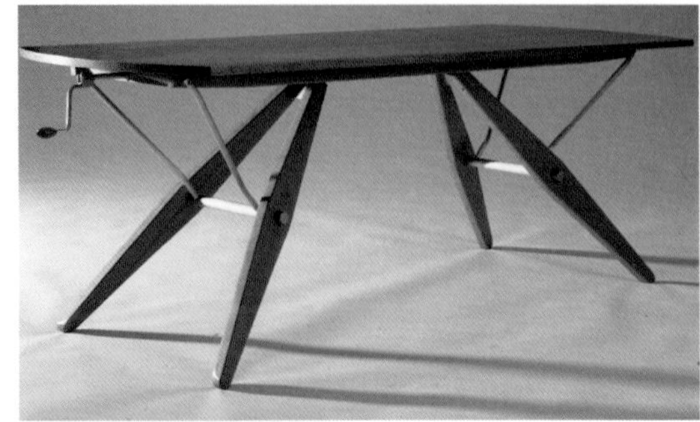

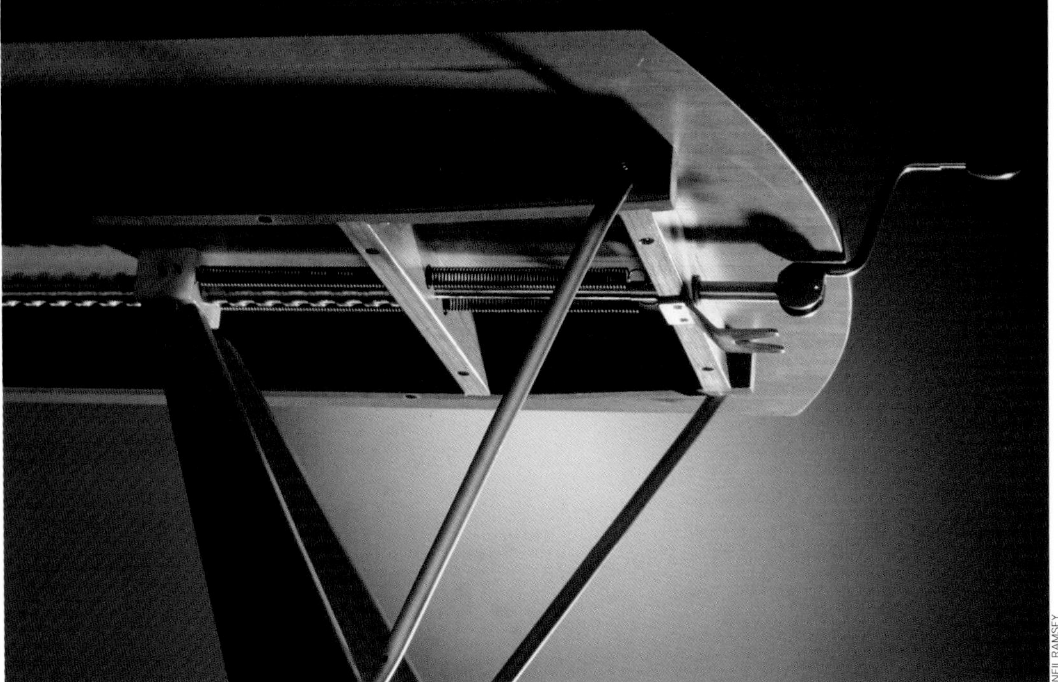

NEIL RAMSEY

"Ease and speed of adjustment, lightweight, portable and controlled" – these are not qualities usually ascribed to a dining table. But according to Michael Kavanagh, all of them apply to *Yo-Yo*, the variable height table he has designed for the Glasgow Collection.

After 20 years as an architect, Kavanagh only recently turned his attention away from buildings towards the objects we place and use within them. The *Yo-Yo* table is one of several designs for furniture developed by his newly founded company, Zebra Design.

A low coffee table that can be raised up to full dining hight, *Yo-Yo* is an ideal item of furniture wherever space is at a premium. Kavanagh, who found available Italian designs along similar lines "awkward" and regarded Japanese equivalents to be "cumbersome affairs", saw an opportunity to expand what he described as "rather a limited market".

The design allows for the controlled, smooth, vertical elevation of the table surface, which remains perfectly horizontal and stable at all times because all four legs maintain contact with the ground during operation (so there is no need to keep clearing away those cups and glasses). *Yo-Yo*'s height is regulated by a mechanism that runs unseen under the tabletop, but the table's function is made clear by the metal crank visible at one end. When it is wound, the tops of all four legs move towards the centre of the table, lowering the table top. Wind the crank in the opposite direction, and the table top is raised.

Funding from the Glasgow Collection allowed Kavanagh to refine previous versions of the design and develop a prototype. A batch of the table's moving parts is already being made, and Kavanagh is experimenting with different materials for the table's surface.

Woven fibre optic wall light

Elaine Bremner

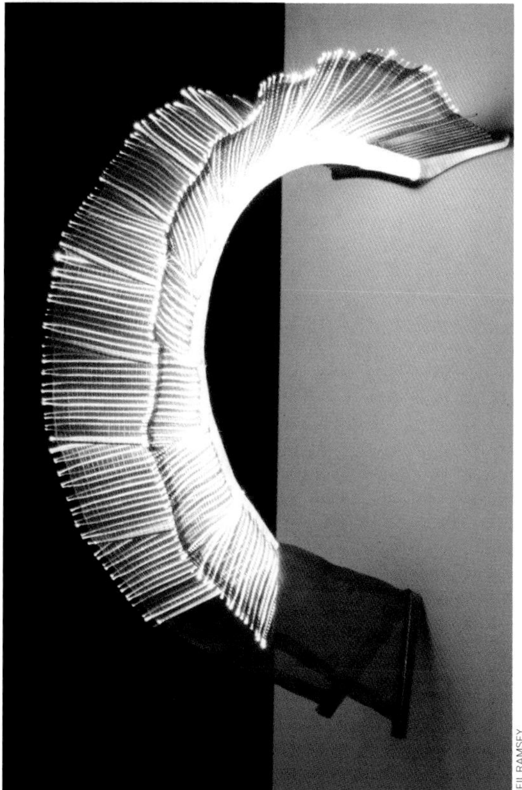
NEIL RAMSEY

Two students spent the summer between their third and fourth years at Glasgow School of Art blurring the borders between textile design and lighting technology. In a collaboration made possible with funding from the Glasgow Collection, textile designer Elaine Bremner and Valerie Lambie of the college's product design engineering department developed a proposed woven light source for *The Lighthouse*, which is now under consideration for use in the newly-refurbished building.

Elaine Bremner made a fabric using copper wire, nylon thread and fine fibreoptic, which she hand-wove "on a very antiquated-looking thing" at the School of Art. To achieve the desired effect, the fibreoptic cables had to be specially prepared before being incorporated in the fabric. "The people who use fibreoptic cables to send information don't want light to escape from them – that only happens when the cables are damaged," Bremner explains. "So we had to investigate how to get the maximum amount of light out of the fibreoptic yarn, and ended up scraping off the surface to let the light through."

The shape of the lamp was inspired by the sculptural curves associated with the work of architect Frank Gehry. The next step involved using paper mock-ups to finalise the lamp's concertina folds before translating them into illuminated metal mesh. Finally, product designer Mike Anusas was brought in to devise a bracket that allows the light to be wall-mounted, with the lightbox, electrical components and bundled ends of the fibreoptic cables hidden from view in a cavity wall.

Snowster Snowboard

Max Berman

The *Snowster* is perhaps the closing chapter to Max Berman's misspent youth. A hybrid made by mixing a sledge and a snowboard, the concept was first dreamed up more than six years ago, when Max was spending all his spare time on his skateboard. When the the ice froze the skater's concrete playground, Berman's thoughts turned to the hills. With the help of a few friends and several "borrowed"plastic signs, he started experimenting with the idea of skating down mountains.

Berman, who now heads his own design company, Imagination for Industry, describes his product as "basically an inexpensive plastic snowboard" through which he hopes to "broaden the sport of snowboarding to a mass market." Made from a single piece of moulded plastic, the key to *Snowster*'s success is its affordability, its availability and its simple design. A typical snowboard costs between £350 and £800, whereas the *Snowster* will have a retail price of around £30. It is designed to be ridden wearing regular shoes, held in place by an adjustable strap and clip; meaning that expensive snowboarding boots and bindings are not needed. Berman hopes that *Snowsters*, unlike regular snowboards which can only be purchased from a handful of specialist shops, will be available from a variety of outlets including toyshops and petrol station forecourts.

With funds from the Glasgow Collection and the Royal Bank of Scotland making possible the testing of a fully-fledged prototype, the *Snowster* will almost certainly be invading a slope near you soon.

ALAISDAIR SMITH

Case study
Seymour Powell and the Linnklok watch
Richard Seymour

We were first approached by Bruce Wood and Deyan Sudjic early in 1998, over a very tasty lunch, with the idea that Seymour Powell might design a product for Linn Products. They asked us whether we would like to choose from one of a number of possibilities: a bicycle, a loudspeaker or a wristwatch. We didn't have to deliberate for long. We had an immediate hunch that the wristwatch – even though it produces no sound – would provide a neat analogy for the company philosophy, and at the same time help Linn diversify into a radically different product area.

In order to make sure that our hunch about the watch was correct, I visited Linn and its director, Ivor Tiefenbrun. Nestling in the green hillsides just outside Glasgow, Tiefenbrun's company is a jewel. It is difficult enough to imagine the far-sightedness which in 1972 led Tiefenbrun to commission the young architect Richard Rogers to design the factory for the company, but once you see it in the flesh, it becomes clear that his visionary approach goes well beyond the acquisition of a piece of early high-tech architecture. A sense of vision and passion pervades the company; Linn is 100% committed to design integrity, and we felt honoured to be invited into the fold.

Inside the factory, Ivor Tiefenbrun showed me devices capable of machining to incredibly small tolerances; precision manufacturing is key to the success of the business. What's more, for Linn the product is not so much the hi-fi equipment, but the quality of the sound that it creates. In other words, the company's product is the accurate reproduction, or representation of sound, using the simplest of means. If the emerging leitmotif was precision and simplicity in sound reproduction, then a wrist watch offered the opportunity to create a perfect analogy to the approach. It should be simple; it should do its job; and it should be committed to delivering its function with a singular purpose – and without any of the nicky nacky noos other watches are stuffed with. In its design philosophy, the wrist watch would thus carry the same genetic imprint as the rest of Linn's range.

Some clients commission a designer and although they may ask for a certain thing – a car, a bike, a chair – in fact what they are looking for is a piece of the person they have approached, and one can think of many products which bear the unmistakeable signature of their designer. Seymour Powell's design philosophy is precisely the opposite of this. We don't set out to 'do a Seymour Powell'; and especially not a 'Dick Powell' or a 'Richard Seymour' (for this project the team was led by James Dawton). In this case, we set out, as it were, to 'do a Linn'.

In terms of manufacturing, we felt that the watch should be a pure and simple object. It would use totally honest materials: a steel case and a strap in leather, but it would utilise them so as to maximise their elegance. As a general principle, Linn's own designers like to conceal fastenings wherever possible, and we mirrored this in the design of the watch by loading the mechanism in through the face, rather than through the more common separate steel back. By doing this, we were able to create the case in the form of a kind of ingot with an extremely smooth underside and absolutely no chance of snagging. The final result is reminiscent of one of those Shepherd's Purse egg-cases which you can find on the beach.

Inside, the wrist watch would contain an automatic

Left: Linn Sondek LP 12
Right: Linn Sondek CD 12

manual mechanism. Since it is intended as an extremely high quality chronograph, we wanted to ensure that maintenance would not be a big issue. By creating a self-winding product without batteries, we could help avoid that dissatisfying moment when you have to witness your trusty timepiece being levered open crudely, exposing it to dust and dirt in the process. This is not to suggest that the Linn wrist watch will never need servicing, but we imagined this to be something carried out in the safe, dust-free atmosphere of Linn's precision watchmakers' workshop rather than over the counter on Sauchiehall Street. Most of all, the elegance of the concept of an automatic watch, wound up by the gentle movement of its wearer and never needing a new battery, seemed to fit with Linn's ideology of simplicity and longevity.

There is nothing temporary about a Linn product. Most people buying hi-fi equipment on, say Argyll Street in Glasgow or Tottenham Court Road in London know, in their heart of hearts, that their brand new CD player probably isn't the last hi-fi they will ever need. Not so with a Linn. Buying a Linn product is rather like walking past the pyramids. This idea of longevity fits neatly with Seymour Powell's own approach (our first rule of recycling is don't). And it fits precisely with the idea of a precision timepiece. It's about time, timelessness, and about doing its job for as long as possible.

One of the surprising things about wristwatch manufacturing is the number of off-the-shelf bits and bobs that are available for use. Boxes of cogs, springs, second hands, and crystals must be stashed in obscure warehouses around Switzerland waiting to be stuffed into someone's supposedly new design. As a result, there's tremendous pressure on watch manufacturers to use existing parts, and the idea of designing a watch absolutely from scratch is not without its problems. We had to struggle to persuade the watch making industry to accept that precision parts needed to be manufactured in the relatively small quantities that would be required in the first instance. Luckily, tenacity is a quality that Linn possesses in bucket loads, and once an initial batch has been made to test the market, it will probably not be long before Linn watches are available in all the same outlets from which their hi-fis can be purchased. The diversification of the company will be complete, and the remit of the Glasgow Collection fulfilled.

The Glasgow Collection initiative has great breadth. In an era when so often things seem to be about money rather than culture, it is exciting to witness an initiative in which culture is seen to have an equal value. Glasgow 1999 has brought a sense of pride to the city, and this awareness that things are happening in Glasgow is of enormous importance, both in the city and outside it. Two things are essential precursors to social change: an idea, and a belief. Ideas without belief don't go anywhere, and Glasgow 1999 is helping to reintroduce self-belief to the city.

The real results of the Glasgow Collection project will not be seen for some years yet, but I honestly believe that already there are signs of a tangible change in attitude. In the past, outside Scotland, it always appeared to be left to comedians like Billy Connolly or Gregor Fisher to maintain the image of a city in decline, but today things are different. It's not so much that the Collection leaves a legacy to the city, because that suggests that the project is already dead. Resolutely alive, the Collection is more like an enzyme, stimulating activity in other parts of the organism, and playing a vital part in its healthy growth.
Richard Seymour is co-founder of Seymour Powell

PETER COOK © LINN PRODUCTS LTD

Designed by Richard Rogers in 1972, the Linn headquarters is located on a 20 acre site at Waterfoot, south of Glagow

Linnklok
Wrist watch

Seymour Powell Associates with Linn Products

Ivor Tiefenbrun, who founded high-end hi-fi manufacturers Linn Products in 1972, is a firm advocate of Albert Einstein's maxim, "Everything should be as simple as possible, but no simpler." So when the firm with a reputation for uncompromising quality linked up with product desigers Seymour Powell, the result was always going to be sleek, exclusive and perfectly engineered.

One of the aims of the Glasgow Collection was to encourage projects and collaborations that would otherwise not have come about, by encouraging established companies to investigate new ways of working, push their technology further or explore different fields and materials. In this case, Linn Products worked with an outside designer and a new manufacturer to develop a product outside their usual area for the first time – the *Linnklok* wrist watch.

"The contact with the Glasgow Collection and Seymour Powell allowed us to tap into both the funding for a speculative endeavour and the creativity of a very talented design consultancy," says Alastair Brown at Linn Products. "Our in-house design department is stretched to the limit as it is, so extraneous projects can sometimes be a problem."

SEYMOUR POWELL ASSOCIATES

With its elegant brushed stainless steel casing and specially developed self-winding watch mechanism, the Linnklok is designed with the company's discerning client base in mind. The first working samples of the watch are now ready, and Linn intends to manufacture a small number which will allow the company to see what the likely uptake of such an item would be. The future of the wrist watch already looks promising: the company aims to sell the *Linnklok* through all Linn's existing retailers, and if all goes well, will distribute it even more widely.

Robbo
Neck guard and baby bib

Jephson Robb, Robbo Company

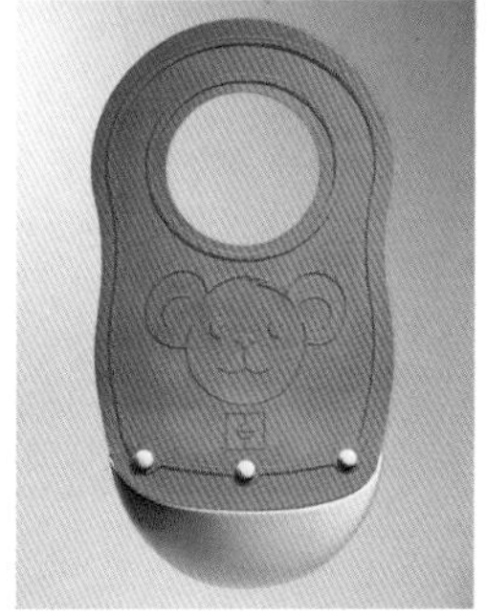

Jephson Robb always hated the fact that getting a haircut also meant getting itchy, uncomfortable bits of hair down his collar. Four years ago, when he was still an economics student, he first had the idea for the *Robbo*, a rubber neck guard with a unique "hairtight" neck seal.

In October 1997, Robb left his financial services job in London to return to Glasgow and set up his own business. "There's no point in having an idea and not doing anything about it," he says now, even though he admits to "not knowing the slightest thing" about the world he was about to enter. Relying on enthusiasm rather than training or experience, Robb did everything himself, from devising the initial design and sourcing materials to manufacture and marketing. He also acknowledges the importance of financial support from the the Glasgow Collection, which enabled him to make his prototype ready for production.

Robbo sold out on its launch at *Salon International*, a hairdressing trade show in Birmingham in October 1998 at which the company was able to be present thanks to a grant from the Royal Bank of Scotland. Today, Jephson Robb has distribution deals across Europe and is looking for more products to develop. The *Robbo children's bib*, which combines the practical benefits of a hard plastic scoop bib with the comfort of a soft rubber neck piece, is his latest venture ("I thought it made sense – there are always more people being born, and that also means more hair that will need cutting.") But it hasn't been easy, from early technical hitches to problems with manufacturers and suppliers. "Friends thought I was mad to give up my job to do this," says Robb. "It's been a lot harder than I thought it would be, but the sense of achievement is phenomenal."

© ROBBO COMPANY

Three legged chair

John Gigli

When John Gigli was laying a new mosaic floor in the foyer of the Glasgow Film Theatre, he heard about plans to refurbish the venue's upstairs bar. He approached the cinema with the idea of developing a stackable chair he had designed as a mature student at Glasgow School of Art in 1998.

Gigli, who continues to operate the building business he established 15 years ago to support his design work and post graduate studies, produced the first two prototypes of his three-legged chair and presented them to the Glasgow Collection. As a result of the meeting, Gigli received funding to pay for the chair to be safety-tested to British Standard level. The Glasgow Collection's seal of approval has also led to funding from the Royal Bank of Scotland, which enabled Gigli to produce a final prototype of his design.

The Glasgow Film Theatre's plans to upgrade its bar may currently be on hold, but they do intend to use a couple of Gigli's chairs for lectures by visiting film makers, panel discussions and publicity purposes.

NEIL RAMSEY

G2V

Treehaus

For an astronomer like Graham Woan, working out the exact position of the sun at any time, in any location, is not a problem. This information lets you predict the path of a shadow cast by any object, an idea that Woan pursued one weekend, just to see what the pattern would look like. The result, a graph made up of a series of curves that indicate the shadow's path for every week in the year, forms the basis for the *G2V* sundial, which takes its name from an astronomer's term for the phase our sun is currently in.

"Conventional sundials are mostly seen as decorative objects of intrigue," says Woan, who lectures on Astronomy and Physics at Glasgow University. "So it surprises people that you can read the time quite accurately from the sun." The *G2V* indicates the right time to within a minute, without having to apply the complicated correction factors previously needed to convert the 'solar time' read from the dial to 'true time'. While this bespoke sundial is only exactly correct in a specific location, all the major population centres in Britain could be well covered with only a dozen different basic models.

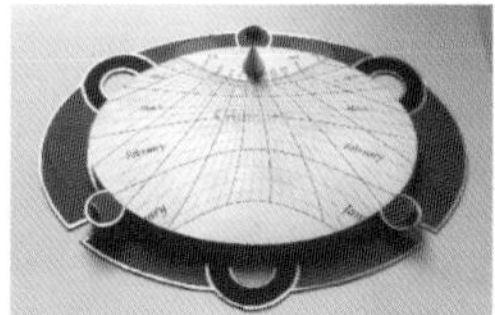

DR GRAHAM WOAN

Woan's own home-made prototype may have consisted of nothing more than a bread board and some nails, but it worked perfectly and demonstrated the concept's potential. The Glasgow Collection set up and funded his collaboration with design partnership Treehaus, which turned his idea into a real product. A grant from the Royal Bank of Scotland paid for the tooling and equipment required to produce the designers' prototype self-assembly sundial, which is made of thick, coated card (Treehaus hopes to produce a more weather-proof metal version soon). All that is required to read the time correctly is to turn the base over at the winter and summer solstices to swap from the autumn to the spring side, and hope for some sunny days.

Concept Q
Vacuum cleaner

IDEO

Even though Hoover enjoys the rare privilege of being mentioned in the dictionary as a generic term, the company felt that Hoover products were no longer perceived to be cutting edge. In order to develop a fresh perspective, Hoover teamed up with California-based design consultancy IDEO to produce a new type of canister vacuum cleaner, known as the *Concept Q*.

The cleaner's controls are located in the handle, including a new function that automatically ejects the plug from the wall socket. An infrared 'Follow me' option can be selected that makes the cleaner body trace the path of the user, like a (well-behaved) dog on a lead. The hose is transparent, making it easier to locate the source of any blockages, and its end can be twisted to clean under furniture. The cleaner is also designed to suit allergy sufferers, with a high level filtration system and a dust vessel that can either be emptied or sent away as a sealed unit for recycling.

George Church, of Hoover's industrial design department, says: "We feel the whole process has gone extremely smoothly. All the parties had very strict timetables and budgets to adhere to, and these were all met. Most importantly, we all consider the design to be very, very good."

This collaboration exemplifies the Collection's role in encouraging companies to move forward with the development of new technology. Hoover will be making a decision on whether to go ahead with production before the end of 1999, but whatever the outcome, it is likely that many of the innovative features developed for *Concept Q* will find their way into Hoover's other vacuum cleaners – all of which are manufactured in Glasgow.

ALAISDAIR SMITH

Highway
Service wall

Esk Furniture Works

ALAISDAIR SMITH

Many office spaces were not designed with modern technology in mind, a situation that is becoming increasingly apparent with greater value being placed on flexibility in the workplace. We want to be able to rearrange the way the office is set up without sacrificing easy access to telephone, computer and power points.

The Esk *Highway* service wall can give new life to old office buildings without having to rip up floors or ceilings to lay new cabling. The system is designed to facilitate the management of space and services by combining the two functions – dividing up the office and delivering the required services to every desktop. The wall's base units, which fit into the dead space below the back of desks, contain the telecommunications and information technology systems without which modern offices cannot function, as well as being able to support partition screens and shelving units as required.

Designed by the Michael Laird Partnership, the service wall is only the second product of a new Scottish manufacturing company set up in 1997 by Tony Walker, an established supplier of high quality imported office furniture products. The first product, an office desking system, was introduced early in 1998, with the service wall system planned to follow later, when the start-up company's funds allowed. By contributing to the prototyping costs, the Glasgow Collection enabled the company to reach this second stage earlier than they had hoped. "Not having this financial support from the Glasgow Collection would have meant delaying the launch of the product a further couple of years," says Simon Laird, the designer responsible for the project. "*Highway* would have lost competitive advantage by not going into production quickly."

Espresso Joe
Mobile espresso cart

Stuart Bailey, ID8

Matthew Algie & Company is the UK's largest producer of roasted coffee, supplying a third of Britain's hotels as well as companies like Marks & Spencer. This family-owned business, founded 136 years ago, has its headquarters in Glasgow and has a long history of supporting the city (including sponsorship of the Glasgow 1999 exhibition *Identity Crisis* at *The Lighthouse*.

The company, which has the contract to open espresso bars in Marks & Spencers stores, had been thinking about producing a mobile coffee vending cart for some time when the opportunity of collaborating with the Glasgow Collection arose. This led to a meeting with product designers ID8, whose approach to producing ergonomically sound products appealed to the coffee company.

Made from high quality materials including stainless steel and Corian, the shapely *Espresso Joe* cart was designed to complement the equally curvaceous *Elektra Barlumé* coffee maker, a top-of-the-range machine made by the people who build Ferrari cars. While the designers ensured that the cart is safe and comfortable to use for the people working behind it, the luxurious, tactile *Espresso Joe* cart is above all inviting to customers. "We wanted people to want to touch it," says Andrew McMillan of Matthew Algie. "*Espresso Joe* is not at all neutral, but it sits happily in lots of different environments." Unlike the plain coffee carts in use in shopping malls or airports, *Espresso Joe* is designed to make you feel good about spending that bit extra for a premium cup of coffee.

Ibis
Textile light screen

DNA and Sue Glasgow

Working with the Glasgow Collection allowed Kim McCormack and Vaishali Londhe of textiles company DNA to try something new. "The initial idea was to develop an innovative piece of contemporary furniture using the same thought processes as those involved in DNA's fabric design," says McCormack. They joined forces with Sue Glasgow, a London-based designer specialising in metals, plastics and lighting, to produce *Ibis* – a sculptural three-part aluminium screen that combines DNA's screen-printed fabrics with innovative lighting technology to create a room divider with its own subtle light source.

McCormack considers the production of the screen's polished cast aluminium frames to have been a crucial stage in the project's development: "The support of the Collection enabled us to produce the pattern for the frame. Each nut, bolt and hinge has been customised to meet the requirements of the piece."

Developing the fabric was no problem – a silk dupion overprinted with "flock" ink to create DNA's trademark overlaid patterns and textures. Getting the light source right proved to be less straightforward. Eventually the team hit upon Prismex, a product by ICI Perspex used for large scale signage. Sandwiched between two layers of fabric, Prismex supplied the even, diffused light effect across the surface of the screens the designers were looking for.

Pohm stor
Storage systems

Helena McGuinness

Glasgow's art schools were the source of many products in the Glasgow Collection. Helena McGuiness may spend a lot of time in the furniture design department at Glasgow's College of Building and Printing, but as a teacher, not a student. Getting involved with the Collection provided a welcome chance to move from theory back into practice.

McGuiness started out by experimenting with the thin translucent plastic that is commonly used for fashionable see-through stationary products. By layering and folding the polypropylene sheets up into boxes and drawers, she quickly found that the light and durable material works surprisingly well in a more domestic context, like storing clothes or small household items. The plastic sheeting's translucent qualities are also very attractive, particularly once you start mixing in coloured plastic for added effect.

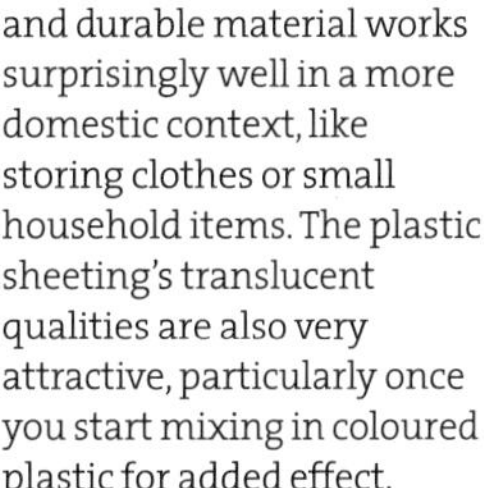

A grant from the Royal Bank of Scotland was put towards tooling costs, and meant an end to the hours McGuiness had previously spent cutting sheets of polypropylene to size by hand with a Stanley knife. The modular plastic units she designed fit into a stainless steel frame clad in translucent panels, making for a very clean, neat and modern look. The *Pohm Stor* modular storage system can be supplied pre-cut and flat-packed, as individual elements or a complete unit, ready to fold, stack and click into place.

HELENA McGUINNESS

Chankey
Key management system

Tony Coffield

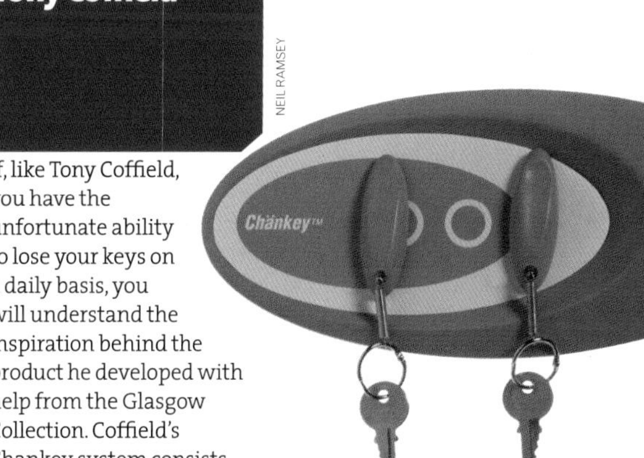

NEIL RAMSEY

If, like Tony Coffield, you have the unfortunate ability to lose your keys on a daily basis, you will understand the inspiration behind the product he developed with help from the Glasgow Collection. Coffield's Chankey system consists of a smart oval base plate and a matching set of small, neat magnetic key rings. "The name derives from the resounding "chank" sound which is created when the key fob meets the base plate," he explains.

Coffield, an interior designer who had "little experience of industrial design" before pursuing his Chankey concept, produced the final design and the prototype with help from Kevin Hughes, a graphic designer. The problems Coffield encountered trying to get his first ever product made were very similar to those of the more recent Glasgow School of Art product design graduates involved in the Glasgow Collection. "Not knowing where to get the right type of expertise for a particular part of prototyping" came near the top of the list of difficulties. But according to Coffield, the link with the Glasgow Collection provided him with much more than just practical information on companies, suppliers and materials. "The Collection has, accidentally or otherwise, become a great source of inspiration and information, especially being able to share experiences with other designers or companies who have encountered similar problems throughout the development of their products."

Since first approaching the Glasgow Collection with his idea in January 1999, Coffield has successfully produced two working prototypes and is now planning the details of the manufacturing process. "All being well the product will be on the market by the end of the year, if not sooner."

Civic giftware

Glasgow School of Art, Product Design Department

When the Glasgow Collection asked product design students at Glasgow School of Art to create Glasgow 1999 souvenirs, they wanted items that did more than commemorate the event – they had to encourage people to actively engage with the festival.

Mark Feely's *Amulet* is a keepsake in the shape of a credit-card sized piece of aluminium with an etched map of Glasgow. Anyone presenting it at festival-related venues could have it stamped to record all the exhibitions and events (and bars) they visited.

Set in square piece of aluminium, Feely's spirit levels are covetable objects that are also aimed at children: while the trapped air bubble of a spirit level holds enough fascination in itself, the instrument also encourages them to explore and test their surroundings.

The curvy shape of Barry McFadyen's silver clip can either be read as a lower case letter g for Glasgow or the number nine.

Craig Glass designed *Hotmetal*, a solid piece of stainless steel that is heated up and then placed on the table to provide a cooking surface for sociable meals. Every item of food cooked on the plate is branded with the Glasgow street grid that is part of the festival's visual identity by MetaDesign.

Left: Spring
Below left: Lolli chair
Below: Scooby

DAVID SPERO

Orrery Coffee table

Yuka Mase

Inspired by the way Chinese dining tables with their central rotating elements are designed to make sharing all the dishes easier, Yuka Mase wanted to bring a practical and sociable element to her *Orrery* table. "I made a comparison with western culture, where people sitting around coffee tables share and pass around things like milk, sugar and biscuits," says Mase. "The main concept of the table is to make sure that it happens smoothly, so there's no need to hesitate before getting something from the other side of the table." The tabletop, made from recycled disposable plastic coffee cups, is shaped like a figure of eight (or the symbol for infinity). True to its name, *Orrery* is orbited by two small satellite side tables, which swivel around the ends of the table. These cast aluminium plates are raised to a comfortable height on which to place cups, even when the table is not being used communally.

Yuka Mase originally studied woven textiles in her native Japan before graduating from Glasgow School of Art's product design department in 1998. The *Orrery* table for the Glasgow Collection, based on a prototype she exhibited at her degree show, was Mase's first commission as a freelance designer. She would like to put it into production, but is looking forward to receiving more feedback on her design once it goes on show. Mase values the support she got from the Glasgow Collection team:

Argyll
Furnishing fabric

Jasper Morrison and Bute Design Studios

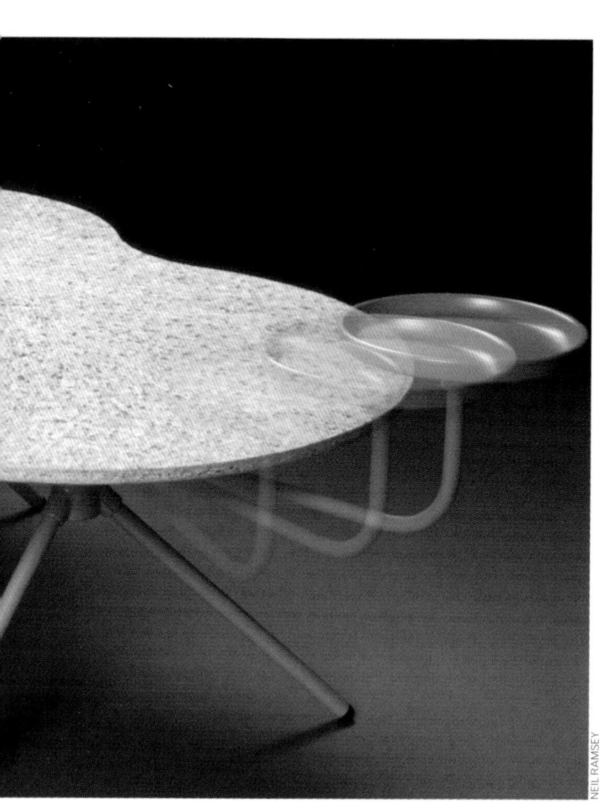
NEIL RAMSEY

"When I got into trouble with the project, they were honest about the good and bad points and talked them through with me. They encouraged me to continue to improve the design."

For a small upholstery textiles company based on a Scottish island, Bute Fabrics are no strangers to unexpected, high-profile collaborations. In 1998, Bute teamed up with London furniture company SCP and five of Britain's best-known furniture designers to produce a small collection of upholstered furniture using fabrics selected from the company's vast library. Apart from providing a showcase for the Bute range, the project allowed the company to get valuable feedback on their fabrics from the designers using them.

For Glasgow 1999, Bute went one step step further, inviting industrial designer Jasper Morrison to design his first ever fabric in collaboration with the company. "The idea was that I would work closely with Jasper, advise on the technical aspects and help interpret his ideas into fabric," says Catherine Murray, Bute's Product Development Manager. From the autumn of 1997 onwards, the first of many samples and ideas were sent back and forth between the Isle of Bute and Morrison's studio in London, with special shades being dyed and colours fine-tuned to the designer's satisfaction.

© BUTE

When Morrison's initial designs, based on solid blocks of colour and large graphic shapes, proved unsuitable for production on Bute's looms, the designer focused on applying his very specific colour ideas to a simple pin dot fabric already in development for the Bute range. Originally conceived as a two-colour weave, the fabric evolved into a three tone version, giving it greater depth and vibrancy, and two separate projects merged into one. As a result, Bute decided to expand the idea of the Glasgow 1999 fabric, which was only envisaged as encompassing five or six colourways, into a large commercial colour range called *Argyll*. Morrison selected a dark, medium and light shade in each of five colours – green, blue, red, beige and grey. An extra brown, a purple and a yellow brought the total number of colourways to 18.

Argyll is primarily intended for contract upholstery use, such as corporate, hospitality and public area seating, but lends itself equally well to high-end residential furniture. The fabric range was officially launched at London's *100% Design* trade fair in 1999. "We are all extremely pleased with the collaboration," says Murray. "The resulting fabric is very simple, precise and elegant, in a very fresh colour story – in fact, very Jasper Morrison!"

Link Link Commercial seating system

The Plan

Marian Whitelaw and Stuart McDonnell, the creative partnership behind Glasgow-based seating and textiles specialists The Plan, aren't afraid of a challenge. Recent achievements include producing 12,000 metres of fabric for a bank's headquarters in the London Docklands, 10,000 metres of printed textiles for the Great Ormond Street Hospital for Sick Children as well as textiles for the newly-refurbished and extended Royal Opera House in Covent Garden. For the Glasgow Collection, they decided to investigate the potential for "a flexible public seating design which did not involve rectangles".

The result was the *Link Link* range of modular seating, inspired by the interlocking links of a bicycle chain. "Financial support from the Glasgow Collection meant that we could concentrate on developing the idea from concept to finished item in a much shorter timescale," says McDonnell, who started working on the project in February 1999. By April, the design was completed, a prototype was ready in June and *Link Link* was officially launched at *100% Design* in London in September 1999.

Each seating module rotates around a vertical cylinder and can be linked to others to form circles, squares, a wide variety of curves and even, if desired, a straight line. Other options currently being explored by The Plan include adding back supports and castors to the individual elements, as well as providing for lighting within the cylinders. The designers believe that, with the appropriate finishes, the system is flexible enough to be used inside or outdoors, in corporate reception areas or bus terminals.

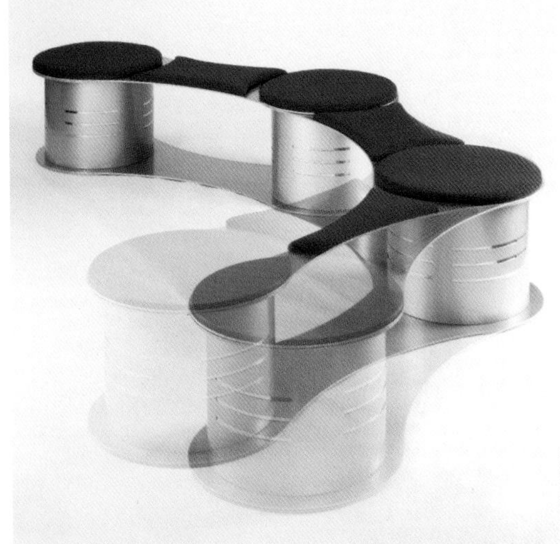

ALAISDAIR SMITH

Bicycle chain lubricator

Primal Design

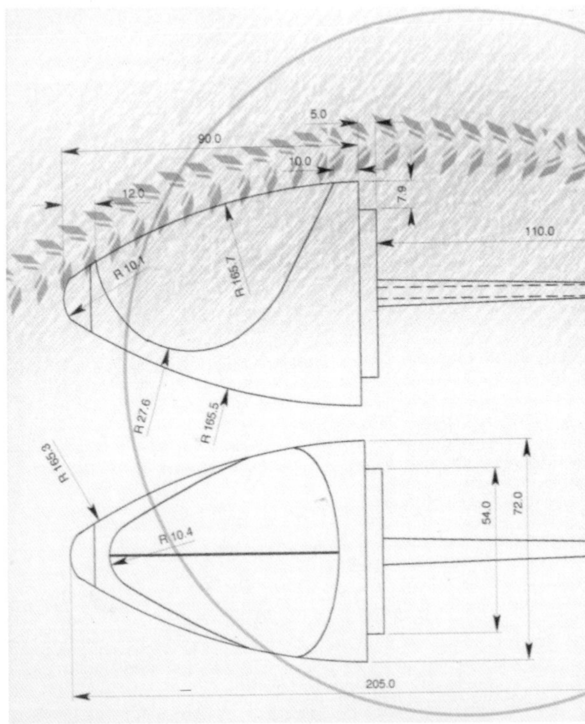

Cleaning bike chains is a necessary but extremely messy and rather tedious chore familiar to anyone who takes their bike remotely seriously. So a system which cleans and lubricates the chain whilst you are riding must be a very good thing.

Glasgow company Scottoilers, who have led the field with their motorcycle chain lubrication system for over ten years, saw an opportunity to move into the bicycle market with a specialist product aimed at keen mountain bikers and road racers. As their system required modifications to work effectively in this new area, the Glasgow Collection put them in touch with Glasgow product designers Primal Design.

© PRIMAL DESIGN

An important difference was that this new version of the system should provide lubrication on demand, rather than a constant supply of fluid. This meant installing a complicated network of wires and plumbing, running along the bicycle frame up to the controls on the handlebars. By squeezing these controls, the cyclist could mix and inject the lubricant (an environmentally sound version not based on mineral oil) into the chain whenever required. Primal Design's main innovation lies in the more efficient placement of the controls: by mounting them on the frame (where less serious cyclists keep their water bottle or the bicycle pump) the connection of all the system's plumbing is made much simpler.

MIKE ANUSAS

Rawlplug hand tool

Mike Anusas

Judging by the ever-increasing number of television programmes and magazines devoted to the subject, the entire nation seems to be obsessed with improving (or at least changing) their homes. One product in the Glasgow Collection might help them achieve a professional result. "The Rawlplug plasterboard punch gives DIYers a simple, accurate way to create holes in plasterboard without having to use an electric drill," says industrial designer Mike Anusas, a graduate of Glasgow School of Art's product design engineering course.

Based on their experiences of the trouble many people have when trying to use plasterboard fixings, Rawlplug's in-house design team recognised an opportunity for a new product. The company approached the Glasgow Collection for help with turning the idea into a working prototype. The project presented an ideal chance for a young local designer to get in on the early stages of the product development process with an established company. "The funding provided by the Glasgow Collection enabled Rawlplug to involve me as part of their design team," explains Anusas, who produced drawings and clay mock-ups of a series of design concepts for the tool's handle. He then made use of the latest digital modelling and rapid prototyping techniques, which were made available by another local company, Thom Micro Systems, to take these initial designs further: "This product allowed Rawlplug to appreciate the benefits of 3D CAD to visualise and prototype designs quickly."

The plasterboard punch is supplied with a selection of cutting heads, designed by Rawlplug's research and development director Campbell Wallace, which match the different sizes of plasterboard fixings the company manufactures. The finished product should be available to eager DIY practitioners in the year 2000.

Delta Chair

Drew Bennett

Considering that many people in residential care homes spend their time sitting in the same chair all day long, surprisingly little thought has been given to designing furniture that addresses their needs. Aware of this situation, Professor Mary Marshall of Stirling University's Dementia Services Development Centre approached the Glasgow Collection with a brief to design a chair specifically for dementia sufferers. She was put in touch with Drew Bennett, and with funding from the Collection, the experienced furniture designer produced a prototype chair designed for maximum comfort.

For the seat of the *Delta* chair, Bennett used a newly-developed soft, heat-sensitive foam that takes on the shape of the person sitting in it, retaining it for a period of time if they leave their seat. The chair back is easily adjustable, as is the pad designed to support the head and neck. Bennett also provided easily accessible storage for anything from magazines to flasks of tea, as well as grips at the front of the arms that help users rise up from the chair. Inspired by similar details Bennett had noticed on Shaker rocking chairs, these mushroom-shaped additions fit the palm of the hand perfectly, encouraging the user to wrap their fingers around them in a soothing grip.

The prototype was lent to a residential care home for "field testing" and feedback, where it was very well received – one lady insisted on thanking Bennett with a kiss. Bennett has already had interest in the chair – now it is just a question of finding a way of producing it at the right price.

DREW BENNETT

Baby feed spoon

XPD

Everyone knows that babies are a high-maintenance addition to the family, it's just that some of the problems that arise are rather unexpected. Making up bottles of milk fomula, for example, would appear to be a straightforward task: first you sterilise the baby's bottles, then you boil the water and leave it to cool. It's the next stage that causes problems – measuring and counting out the scoops of baby feed. Keeping track of anything up to 54 scoops of milk powder when making up six bottles of feed is hard enough at the best of times, but just counting up to seven proves virtually impossible if you are also trying to cope with constant interruptions and chronic sleep deprivation at 3am.

Following the birth of her child in 1996, Kirsty Hall decided to try and help other new parents experiencing similar difficulties by developing a product that would "take the baby formula powder from its tin, measure it accurately and keep track of how many scoops have been put into each bottle."

In order to help Hall turn her idea into a fully-functioning product, the Glasgow Collection funded her collaboration with Newcastle-based company XPD, winners of a design award for Best Nursery Product in 1998.

For Kirsty Hall's baby feed spoon, XPD developed a mechanical solution to the problem they were set. With every 'scoop', the user pushes a plastic ridge in the spoon's handle forward with their thumb to automatically level off the amount of powder. This action also activates a counting mechanism, which indicates the number of 'scoops' added on a clear, easy to read scale on the handle.

The spoon, which is easy to operate using either the right or left hand, can also be taken apart for cleaning. This makes it easy for parents to keep up their standards of hygiene, in spite of powdered baby formula's tendency to find its way into tiny gaps and and stick to plastic surfaces.

ALAISDAIR SMITH

Sonus Amplifier

Factory Design

Working with the Glasgpw Collection has allowed Sonus Engineering to produce an amplifier with a casing that is as radical a departure from their previous products as the technology inside it. "Until Bruce Wood suggested it, we hadn't even considered working with a design company," says Tam Lynch, who with his wife is responsible not only for the electronics of all other Sonus products, but also their marketing and distribution. The collaboration was also supported by grants from the Royal Bank of Scotland and economic funding agency Glasgow North.

Sonus started developing the electronics for the amp, which is capable of reproducing a much more comprehensive and responsive range of sounds than similar products, four years ago. Previously, they had designed all their cases themselves, and admit to finding the design process more difficult than expected. "The designers' ideas were excellent, but some turned out to be a nightmare to manufacture," says Lynch. "It's been an eye-opening experience."

Designed by a young London-based product design company called Factory, the casing can be customised to suit different tastes. Factory worked closely with Sonus to source, order and define prototype parts. Apart from its unconventional looks, the amplifier is also a departure from the other Sonus products in that it is designed for greater ease of manufacture. Once the amp goes into full production at the end of 1999, Sonus will be able to sell it at a much better price than the specialist equipment they previously made in very small runs.

© FACTORY DESIGN LTD

Low Table

Dene Happell

As first customers for a brand new product go, the new Glasgow branch of London's well-established Groucho Club isn't bad. But the *Low* table wasn't the only contribution Dene Happell made to Groucho Saint Judes: he was also responsible for the lighting in the entrance and the tables in the downstairs bar. The commission wasn't even his first brush with the world of fashionable drinking establishments: in August 1998, he designed the interior (and almost everything in it) for acclaimed Glasgow bar Air Organic.

The *Low* table is at home in any situation, and can be adapted to its environment and the needs of its users. The table revolves, allowing easy access to built-in storage compartments and items on the table top. Together with ceramics specialists Fireworks (whose own *Porcini* tableware is also part of the Glasgow Collection), Happell developed a selection of ceramic inserts, including a bowl, a vase, an ashtray and a wine cooler, that slot into the main body of the table, instantly changing its feel and function.

Happell graduated from Glasgow School of Art's sculpture department in 1994, and worked as a film maker and artist before setting up his interior and furniture design business in May 1998. "Assistance from the Glasgow Collection has offered me the opportunity to develop the table to a stage where it can enter the marketplace successfully," says Happell, who launched *Low* at *100% Design* in London in September 1999. "With their support I was in a position to approach several manufacturing companies who have subsequently been able to provide me with a finished product."

House light family Lamps

Nicolai Moe

Nicolai Moe's lights look like a cross between a car headlamp and an origami project, with an added hint of iMac thrown in. But on closer inspection, it's their startlingly simple but effective construction that really stands out.

Moe started developing his novel range of friendly light-weight lamps in his final year of a product design course at Glasgow School of Art. Funding from the Glasgow Collection allowed him to work up his concepts into fully functioning, versatile prototypes that look good whether they're hung from the ceiling or propped up on a table.

The two-tone lamps are constructed using two identically shaped sheets of thin flexible polymer, one brightly coloured and the other milky white and translucent, but both bearing the same graphic pattern, be it a geometric grid or a series of wavy lines. When gently folded and snapped together at their zig-zagged edges, the two sheets combine to create a striking, simple three-dimensional shape. Rather than attempting to cover up the joins where the clear and coloured materials meet, Moe turned these interlocking seams into an integral part of the design. Moe, who moved back to his native Norway after graduating, is currently investigating the possibility of turning his *House Light Family* into a commercially viable product.

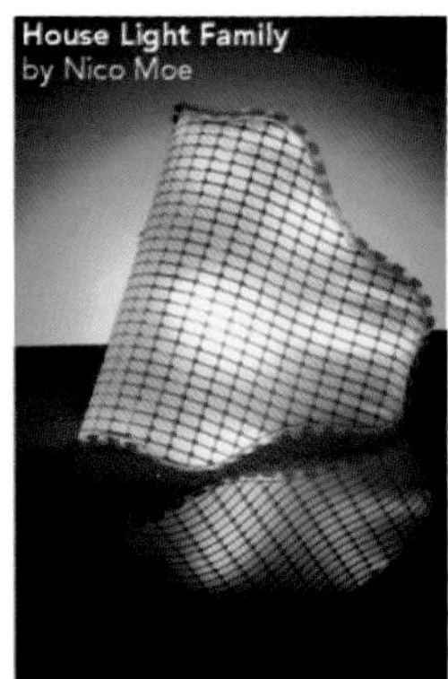

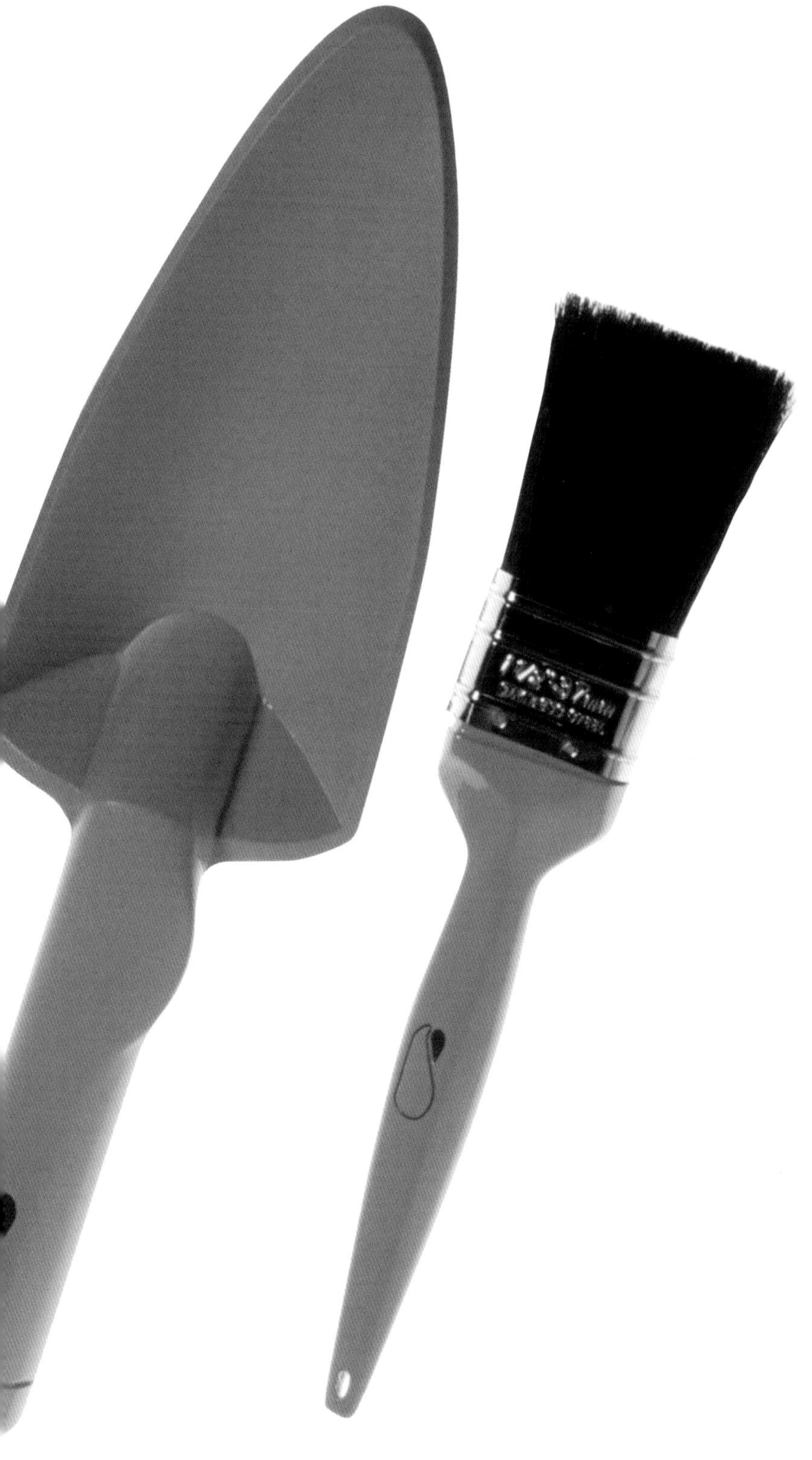

Rotilt
Ergonomic grip handles

Designed by Stuart Bailey, ID8

When dentist Glen Heavenor set out to develop a better toothbrush, he ended up making a significant development in ergonomics instead, without even realising it at first. The result of his experiments with dental putty was the *Rotilt* handle, which gives people an easier and more natural way of rotating implements by making more use of the thumb. The handle allows the user to change his grip gradually, without putting strain on the wrist or resorting to awkward arm postures. It is also unusual in being suitable for both left – and right-handed users.

The Glasgow Collection put Heavenor in touch with design consultants ID8, and funded their work to produce a computer model of the handle that would enable them to produce moulds and prototypes. "I thought a proper designer would take my design and change it completely," says Heavenor. "But it was more a case of capturing the basic geometry of my example, and then tidying it up." Obvious prototype applications for the handle included items like gardening tools and paintbrushes, but pushing his four-year-old son around Eurodisney last summer provided Heavenor with the inspiration for what has so far proved to be the most successful use of his design: a stroller. More chance encounters and some further development work later, Heavenor ended up with a licencing agreement with Mothercare. A range of buggies equipped with *Rotilt* handles should be in stores around Britain for January 2000.

Heavenor is convinced that *Rotilt* will eventually be taken up by the toothbrush manufacturers that initially turned him down. In the meantime, he has taken out patents around the world, thought of dozens of other potential uses for his idea and is hoping to quit dentistry for good in two years time. "It's amazing," says Heavenor. "Three years ago, I hardly knew what ergonomics was. Now I'm on the Ergonomics Council."

Homes for the Future

One Foot Taller, lwd, Adrian Wiszniewski

Below left: Canyon lounge chair by One Foot Taller Right: furniture by lwd Far right: rug by Adrian Wiszniewski

One of the lasting legacies of Glasgow 1999 is *Homes for the Future*, over 100 flats and houses designed by leading architects for a previously derelict site on Glasgow Green. During the summer of 1999, the then still uninhabited *Homes* were opened to the public.

Much more than just another housing development, the project offered an ideal opportunity to think about the way we live. Eleven designers, architects and artists from Glasgow and beyond were asked to respond to the wide range of unfulfilled housing needs and desires that came to light in a unique survey commissioned by Glasgow 1999. The concept products and interiors they produced were installed in houses around the site, resulting in a series of room sets a world away from the chintzy soft furnishings and bland colour schemes of the average show home. Three of the products developed as part of this project are represented in the Glasgow Collection.

Canyon, the lounge chair by One Foot Taller, is best described as a curvy, low-slung cousin of *Chasm*, the design duo's award-winning rotation-moulded plastic chair which is also part of the Glasgow Collection (page xx). Here, the innovation lies in the design's modular structure: individual elements can be combined to form a basic armchair or a large sofa.

Sam Booth of Glasgow-based design company lwd developed a range of light-weight furniture including a dining table and bookshelves. All the furniture is easy to pack up and carry away – ideal for anyone in the habit of moving house (or rearranging the contents of their living room) on a regular basis.

Artist Adrian Wiszniewski brought his vibrant colours and graphic style into the living room on a grand scale. His contribution to the Glasgow Collection consists of a large rug manufactured by the Edinburgh Tapestry Company that reproduces the bold squares of his painting 'Well Hung'.

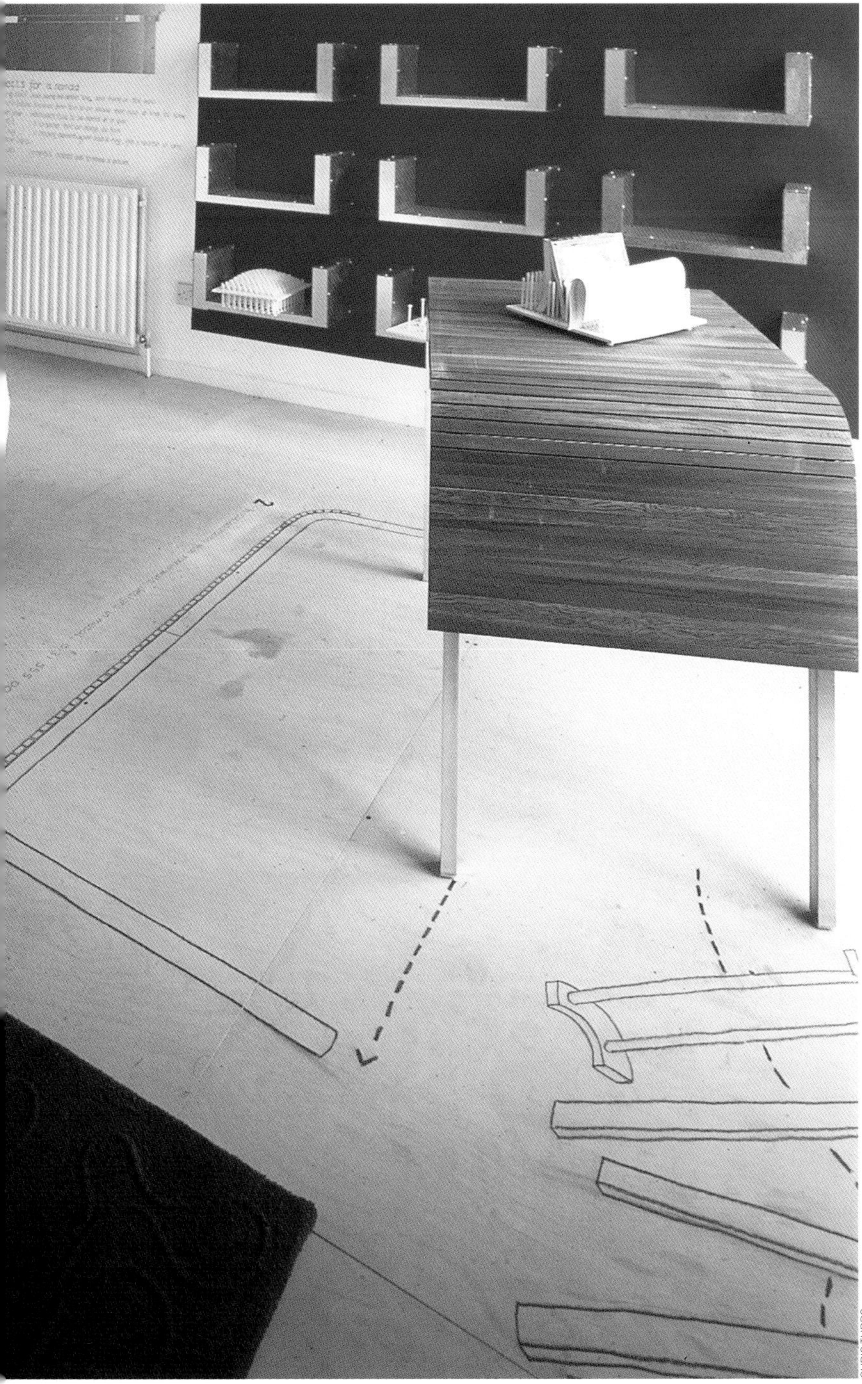

CHRIS TUBBS

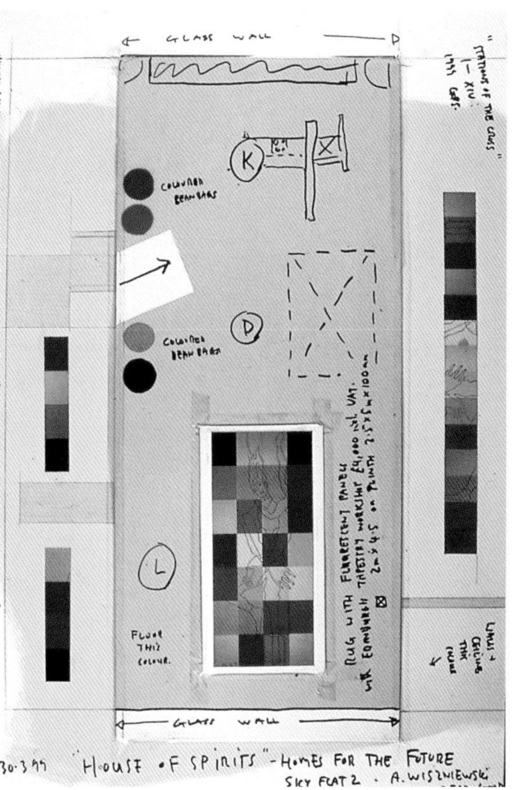
GLASS WALL
COLOURED BEAN BAGS
COLOURED BEAN BAGS
FLOOR THIS COLOUR.
GLASS WALL
30.3.99 "HOUSE OF SPIRITS" - HOMES FOR THE FUTURE
SKY FLAT 2 . A. WISZNIEWSKI

Case study

Please Touch adds an extra dimension to the Glasgow Collection's principal criteria of innovation and commercial viability. Inviting artists to work with furniture company SCP to design and prototype seven pieces of furniture, Please Touch brings together the disciplines of fine art and industrial design.

Fiona Bradley

The artists involved in Please Touch – Martin Boyce, Michael Craig-Martin, Dorothy Cross, Andrew Miller, Julian Opie, Richard Wentworth and Rachel Whiteread – are all makers of objects and users of the vocabulary of furniture in their art. In commissioning them as part of the Glasgow Collection, however, independent curator Edmund Hubbard asked them to work entirely within the rhetoric and practice of product design. Sharing an interest in the different context for which objects may be made, and in how those contexts define an individual work, each of the artists has used this project to develop the posibility that some of their ideas may be more successful as furniture than art.

Some of the artists' furniture – Whiteread's daybed, Miller's table, Opie's sofa, Boyce's chair – uses ideas gleaned from the practice of furniture design to develop a proposition that they had previously investigated within their art. Wentworth's stool and Craig-Martin's sofa/table are less specifically related to their practice as artists, but use the process of product design to extend their usual ways of interrogating and understanding the world. Cross's bed marks the artist's decision not only to make furniture for the first time, but also to work for the first time with text, using the opportunity provided by the furniture commission to explore the new possibilities of both.

The activity of these artists has key precedents in twentieth century art, notably the furniture designed by Donald Judd which was instrumental in his development of a type of art which could be described as 'three dimensional work' rather than either painting or sculpture. Made as furniture, but not intended as an entry into the marketplace of design, Judd's objects tested his ideas in relation to a new set of limitations and possibilities. His use of furniture as a vehicle for the exploration and development of ideas (albeit ideas belonging to the history of art) was in turn supported by the history of modern design. The classic modernist equation of form with function is one of the abiding ideas and ideals of the twentieth century, while the utopianism inherent in much design theory is based on finding common ground between various visual practices: 'the object of all creative effort in the visual arts is to give form to space' (Walter Gropius, 1923).

Despite this apparent similarity, however, art continues to be art and furniture furniture. All of the artists involved in this project were concerned to make something which could be used, and something whose form was intimately linked to that use. In this, they approached the rigour of classic modernist designers such as Ray and Charles Eames, but the ideal of use as manifested in the artists' objects seems closer to a potential for narrative than to a modernist understanding of function. Made to be occupied by the body, its form defined in the present by the demands made by assumed future use, the artists' furniture nevertheless hints at something more. Intimately concerned with what all furniture is, the artists' prototypes suggest a little of what this furniture could be.

Please Touch
Artists furniture commissions

Martin Boyce
Chair (noir)

Martin Boyce's adjustable *Chair (noir)* is simple, even basic. Although the punched steel of the legs resembles perhaps the brackets of a shelving system, or even the uprights from an Eames storage unit, the chair's references are few. Mostly, it looks like a chair or, perhaps more accurately, a sign or signal for a chair. When you sit on it, it feels like a chair, albeit one which plays with discomfort. In the course of designing it, the artist discovered that chairs are made with comfort ratings. Some places do not want you to sit down for long, and this chair perhaps belongs in one of those. It adjusts without reference to the human body, only the back sliding up and down. This betrays the chair's true function and, in turn, its meaning: it is not meant only to be sat on, but rather has been designed to fit snugly underneath any door handle, to act as a wedge or barricade.

Recently, the artist has shown a series of photographs of different chairs, all modernist design classics, used to wedge a door closed. The camera angle barricades the viewer into the room with the chair. Frozen in a moment of cinematic narrative clarity, each photograph is charged with menace.

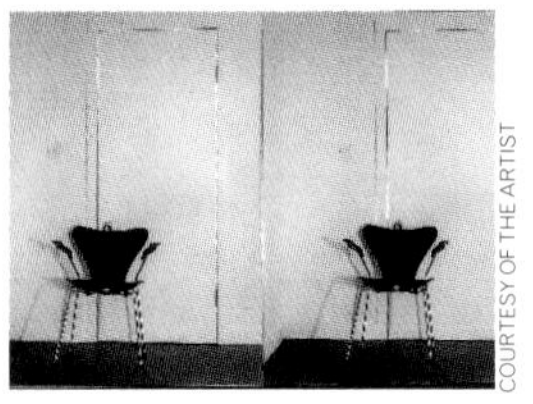

COURTESY OF THE ARTIST

Above: Martin Boyce, *Double Black Disaster (In Advance)* (1999)
Below: Chair (noir)

This menace has the familiarity of a film noir classic, mixed with the sense that we surely have, or might have, once done this ourselves with a chair. Chairs are useful for many more things than sitting on – they make good impromptu tables and step ladders, supports and weapons. In taking the chair out of the photographs and remaking it according to its function within them, Boyce has reversed the accustomed order of things so that one of a chair's useful auxiliary functions has become its main purpose.

In doing this, Boyce engages both with the ways in which in general we use and misuse furniture. The chair is the epitome of classic design – each famous designer has their signature chair. The chairs in Boyce's photographs are of this type, articulating the ideas of their designers in their purest form. Conceived of by those designers as affordable, democratic and utopian, however, the signals sent now by the chairs of the Eames and of Jacobsen are those of exclusivity, 'good' taste and financial affluence. Much of Boyce's work concerns the changing relationship of classic design to public consumption and the culture of the designer interior. This present chair is in dialogue with this relationship and with the artist's own examination of it.

Michael Craig-Martin
Sofa/bed/table/desk/shelving

Rather than using this project as a way of taking forward a particular idea developed in his artistic practice, Michael Craig-Martin has instead seized the opportunity to design an object that he wants himself. Motivated primarily by desire, he has made a piece of furniture which is both extremely flexible and rather didactic – anticipating its future owner's every domestic need, it also suggests modes of behaviour that the owner may not yet have considered.

A large table with a bite taken out of it, the piece combines a sofa which is also a single bed, with a dining table which is also a desk with shelving underneath. Designed for single ownership (the artist speaks of it as furniture for a bedsitter, made for himself in terms of what one person needs) and to be the principal, if not the only furniture in a room, it nevertheless encourages both solitary and social activity. Oscillating between passive accommodation and active suggestion, the *Sofa/bed/table/desk/shelving* articulates the subtle tyranny of domestic objects. The furniture we

COURTESY OF THE ARTIST AND TATE GALLERY

have inevitably conditions the way we behave, and being able to do something because our furniture allows it can swiftly become a habit that the furniture won't allow us to break.

Craig-Martin is interested in furniture as the double embodiment of human activity; made both by and for someone. In his view, a chair looks like a chair because of what it has to do rather than as the result of a design decision.

With much in common with the current trend towards multi-use, flexible domestic furniture in contemporary design, Craig-Martin's *Sofa/bed/table/desk/shelving* is essentially a series of overlapping practical activities and interconnected experiential possibilities. Shifting around between sleeping, working, sitting and entertaining, it begins, like much of the artist's other work, with the conventional connections of object to activity before sliding out from underneath its received definition to make its occupant think, and act, again.

Left: Michael Craig-Martin, *Four identical boxes with lids removed* (1969) Below: *Sofa/bed/table/desk/shelving*

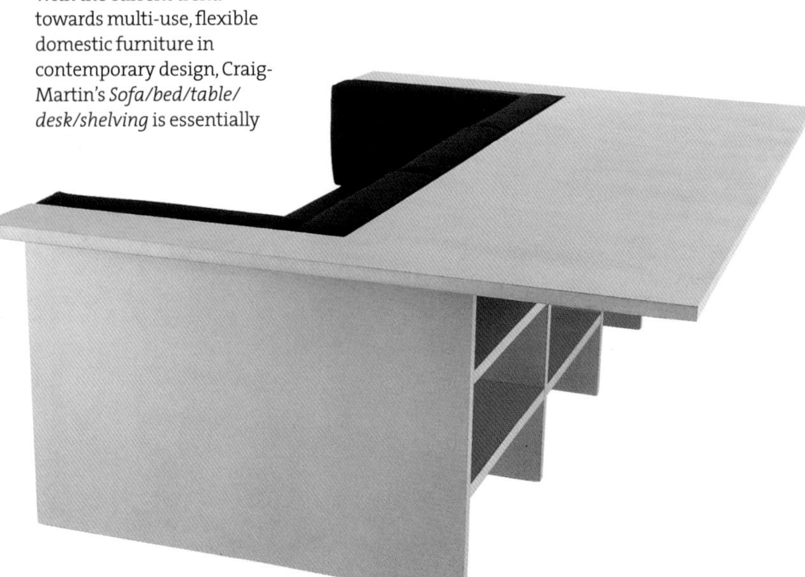

Dorothy Cross Lit-bed-leaba

Dorothy Cross's *Lit-bed-leaba* is a simple wooden bed made from a slatted base on square legs, with a roll of white felt to go between it and a mattress. Carved into the slats of the base is an extract from a text by Marguerite Duras, The Man Sitting in the Corridor (1991).

The text was the starting point for the artist's design of the bed and provides a key to its meaning both as a piece of furniture and in relation to Cross's artistic practice. It describes, in breath-takingly erotic yet tender detail, a woman sucking a man's penis.

When the artist first encountered the text, it had already been translated from French into English. She had it re-translated it into Irish, using the old Gaelic alphabet she hadn't used since school. The deliberate obscurity of the language turns the text into a beautiful thing to be looked at rather than understood, and responds to the obscurity of the erotic imagination and memory.

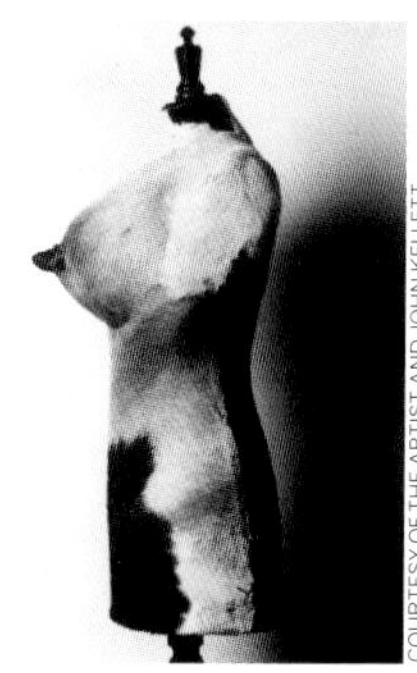

COURTESY OF THE ARTIST AND JOHN KELLETT

Above left: Dorothy Cross, *Amazon* (1993)
Left: Lit-bed-leaba

COURTESY OF THE ARTIST

Above: Andrew Miller, *Breakfast Bar* (1999)
Right: *One on One*

Duras' prose, a witness and perhaps also an incitement to sexual arousal, is obscured through linguistic trickery and then hidden under the mattress.

The carved lettering, lying innocent in its unreadability under the mattress, animates the bed with the possibility of future action. Dormant until the bed is occupied, it will then impress itself into the white felt lying like a printer's blanket above it.

Andrew Miller
One on One

Of all the artists participating in this project, Andrew Miller is the one most accustomed to making furniture. His *One on One*, a trestle table made from a heavy sheet of sandblasted patterned glass and two hardwood bases, is directly related to an artistic practice primarily concerned with the interrogation of furniture and its domestic or public function.

The table re-uses an idea from 1993, when the artist became interested in using readily-available objects as the basis for sculpture. *One on One* imagines a table held up by a pair of 'free agents'; trestles that might twist and turn away from one another just as easily as squaring up in direct confrontation.

Of course Miller's trestles are not really free to act independently, but rather in dynamic relation to one another. To keep the table a table, each must respond to the other's movements. The title of the piece borrows from the terminology of basketball, a sport in which players mark each other one on one, keeping pace with each other's shifts and tricks. This reference is repeated in the table top, which is made of glass so that the antics of the bases may be clearly seen. The glass is patterned in a rectangular area reminiscent of the markings of a basketball backboard with the hoop removed.

Most of the artist's other furniture has been made for art contexts; shown either in galleries as art objects or made specifically as gallery furniture. Recently, however, he has been interested in relinquishing control of the reception of his work, making furniture for individual homes or for public spaces. The art work, rather than being the piece of furniture itself, becomes the photograph the artist takes of it in its new home. *One on One*, made to be taken away and used without reference to the artist's intentions for it, is an extension of this practice.

Julian Opie
Tube Station

COURTESY OF THE ARTIST AND LISSON GALLERY, LONDON

Julian Opie's *Tube Station*, made from upholstered foam tubes of different diameters zipped together, looks provisional and somewhat unstable. It seems amorphous until sat on, whereupon it proves perfectly stable and surprisingly comfortable.

The sofa is a development, in the form and context of furniture, of the ideas inherent in a sequence of sculptures Opie made around 1991. Columns formed out of complex moulded architraves, the surfaces of these objects wound tortuously in and out, rising above the viewer so that it was impossible to seek an understanding of their structure by looking at them in another way – horizontally for example, or in section.

The sofa is an attempt to return in a different way to the structure of the column sculptures, this time offering an immediately available alternative view: from sideways on the complex tubular construction reveals itself clearly in section.

Although the sofa is formally connected with Opie's column sculptures, as a sofa it overlaps with the history and tradition of furniture as well as the history of Opie's art. Opie believes that its function as furniture is the first thing it should communicate. The meaning of art objects is made in art galleries, while a sofa begins to work as it is sat on. Part of this sofa's meaning, however, is that there is no correct way to sit on it – Opie wonders whether sofas may perhaps be a little too prescriptive, and wants his to involve a certain amount of imagination and improvisation. In this, *Tube Station* is a starting point and shares a certain kinship with those of his sculptures that invite imaginative activity and participation: *Imagine you are walking*, 1993; *Imagine you can order these*, 1993; *You are in a car*, 1996; *You see an office building*, 1996. You are now in an exhibition of furniture. Imagine you are sitting.

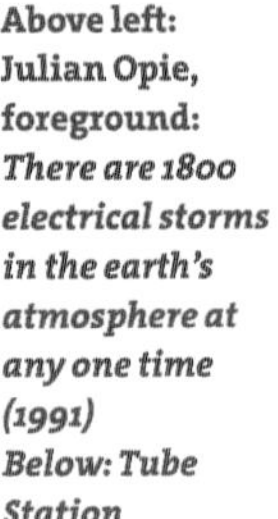

Above left: Julian Opie, foreground: *There are 1800 electrical storms in the earth's atmosphere at any one time* (1991)
Below: *Tube Station*

Richard Wentworth
Cleat

Richard Wentworth's *Cleat* is inspired by the artist's personal relationship to objects in the home. Wentworth delights in a haphazard accumulation of things and in the role that chance plays in the way in which objects find their way into most interiors. Domestic objects have an innate narrative – they have a point of origin and a different, designated 'home'.

Cleat is modelled on the device used for securing ropes on board a ship. Different in shape from quay-side bollards used to tie boats to on land, such cleats are available for all vessels from rowing boats to ocean liners, and range from the tiny to the huge. Wentworth's adoption and adaptation of a nautical cleat was inspired by its innate mobility – it is designed to put to sea. The artist uses this as an index both for the functional mobility of the stool it becomes (the French word for furniture, meuble, also means 'mobile' and of all items of furniture stools tend to move around the most) and the conceptual and categorical mobility of the found object, whose importance in art history he quotes. *Cleat* is in many ways a rebuttal of the central

importance of the found object in the history of twentieth century art.

The found object in the language of modernism depends on a change of context to be meaningful as art. Deliberately mobile, *Cleat* has no pre-determined context. Wentworth has made a stool from a cleat by announcing that is what he has done and issuing an invitation to sit. Although its shape has been modified, it is as much of cleat as one still on board a ship, which would, if sat on, be just as much of a stool.

Wentworth's work as a sculptor is concerned with a gathering of objects and the ways in which they may be looked at and understood. Naming and renaming of objects plays a major part in his practice, not in order to rupture the connection between practicality and possibility, but to extend it. Much of his sculpture plays on a kind of domestic paranoia – if we call it by something other than its name, will we still know what it is? *Cleat* partakes of this, retaining enough of its original identity perhaps even to cease being a stool when not in use.

Above: *Cleat*
Below: Richard Wentworth, *Basel 1997* (From *Making Do & Getting By* series)

Above right: Rachel Whiteread, *Untitled (Black Bed)* (1991)
Below right: *Day bed*

COURTESY OF THE ARTIST AND NISSON GALLERY, LONDON

Rachel Whiteread
Daybed

COURTESY OF THE ARTIST AND ANTHONY D'OFFAY GALLERY, LONDON

Rachel Whiteread has made an upholstered daybed, a classic object in the canon of modernist design. While its form inevitably refers to this, it has more to do with Whiteread's own practice than with furniture design, and this is betrayed by its minimal detailing. The four holes in the corners and the regular bumps and depressions stitched into the surface signal its designer's interest not so much in the object itself, but in its relationship to another, similar object.

Whiteread is known for her casts of the spaces in, under or on everyday objects. She takes direct casts from beds, chairs, tables, bookcases and wardrobes, investigating the familiar domestic landscape of things designed by humans for human use. The daybed is closely related to a group of sculptures which explore the space underneath a simple bed in casts made from plaster or rubber. To understand them, the viewer needs mentally to reconstruct a bed around them, slotting legs into the holes and imagining the sprung construction up against which the cast material pushes.

The daybed invites the viewer to lie down, but is less comfortable than a real bed, denying the possibility of a long, nocturnal sleep. The source of its lack of comfort – the holes and the stitching – betrays its conceptual origins in art, and begins a chain of associative speculations. Lying on the daybed, the viewer is in fact lying on the materialisation of the space underneath another bed, occupying in person the space where the actual bed would have been.

Whiteread's bed sculptures entail imaginary occupancy, fantasised returns to beds we have known. Physically occupying the daybed, however, the viewer is enticed onto the space whose emptiness inspired its solid form. Whiteread's sculptures are indications of an absent presence – furniture whose existence persists only in memory. This daybed forces one such memory to assume a very present absence; a tangible, usable form.

Ursula stainless steel bath tub
Chasm chair
Ravine dining chair
Fine Bone China Lamp
Solo flat pack clock
Open Museum display system
Pup laminated furniture range
Glasgow 1999 Luminaire

Bop light
Skins digital hand drum
Leather Bags
Contemporary ceramics
Recycled plastic furniture
Quentin paper pulp lamp
Uma paper pulp lamp
First aid and eye wash dispensers
Linnklok watch
Robbo neck guard and baby bib
Hidden 'til lit

Dante portable gas heater
Spring, Scooby and Lolli children's furniture
Porcini, Exo vessel and Haiku plate ceramic tableware
Concept canal barge
Exhibition system
Yo-Yo height adjustable table
Woven fibre optic light
Snowster
G2V sundial
Concept Q vacuum cleaner
Highway service wall
Espresso Joe mobile coffee cart
Ibis textile light screen
Pohm stor storage system
Chankey key management system
Civic giftware
Orrery table
Argyll furnishing fabric
Rotilt ergonomic grip handles
Rawlplug hand tool
Bicycle chain lubricator
Baby feed spoon
Link Link commercial seating
Delta chair
Sonus amplifier
Low table
House Light Family lamps
Three-legged chair
Vortex crab claw dinghy sail
Three Homes for the Future products
Please Touch artists furniture

Submarine
One Foot Taller

Fireworks
Arkitype Design Partnership
Timorous Beasties
Graven Images
McKeown Alexander
Gerry Taylor
VK&C Partnership
Ben Smith, Digital Cow
Frank Gallacher
Yam Design

Paul Pearson
Jules Goss
Wallace Cameron Group
Seymour Powell Associates
Jephson Robb
Fitch
Crombie Anderson Associates
Kirsten Hough
Craig Whittet

Zoo Architects
Iwd
Michael Kavanagh, Zebra Design
Elaine Bremner
Max Berman
Treehaus
IDEO California
Michael Laird Partnership
Stuart Bailey, ID8 Ltd
DNA and Sue Glasgow
Helena McGuinness
Tony Coffield
Craig Glass, Mark Feely and Barry McFadyen
Yuka Mase
Jasper Morrison and Bute Design Studio

Mike Anusas
Primal Design
XPD
The Plan
Drew Bennett
Factory Design Ltd
Dene Happell
Nicolai Moe
John Gigli
Adrian Shields
Adrian Wieszniewski
Michael Craig-Martin, Dorothy Cross, Andy Miller, Julian Opie, Richard Wentworth, Rachel Whiteread and Martin Boyce

Millennium Products: Product awarded Millennium Product status

The Royal Bank of Scotland: Project supported by The Royal Bank of Scotland

manufactured by Associated Metal (stainless), Glasgow
for NiceHouse Ltd, Glasgow, manufactured by Dip Mouldings, Irvine
for NiceHouse Ltd, Glasgow
specified in Strata, a bar in Glasgow's Queen Street
for The Lighthouse
laminates by Novograf, furniture manufactured by Morris, Glasgow

manufactured and designed by Philips Lighting Ltd for the National Stadium, Hampden

in association with David Bernard,Sound Surgery

supported by British Polythene Industries
manufactured by Universal Pulp Packaging

manufactured by Wallace Cameron Group
for Linn Products
manufactured by the Robbo Company
2D design concepts for McGavigans, Glasgow, with funding from Scottish Design Ltd

in association with Strathclyde University British Waterways
for The Lighthouse, Glasgow

in association with Valerie Lambie and Mike Anusas

for Dr Graham Woan, Dpt of Physics & Astronomy, Glasgow University
for Hoover European Appliance Group
manufactured by Esk Furniture Works Ltd
for Matthew Algie & Company Ltd
supported by ICI Perspex

for Glasgow City Council

for Bute Fabrics
for Glen Heavenor
for Rawlplug
for Scottoilers
for Kirsty Hall

in collaboration with Dementia Services Development Centre, Stirling
for Sonus Engineering, with additional funding from Glasgow North

for Glasgow 1999's Homes for the Future project
manufactured by SCP

Glasgow 1999
UK City of Architecture and Design

Glasgow 1999 management team
Deyan Sudjic, Director
Eleanor McAllister, Depute Director
Nicole Bellamy, Exhibitions Director
Pauline Gallagher, Community Initiatives Director
Sarah Gaventa, Communications Director
Andrew Gibb, Development Director
Gordon Ritchie, Marketing Manager
Anne Wallace, Education Officer
Bruce Wood, Glasgow Collection Director

Glasgow Collection Team
Bruce Wood, Glasgow Collection Director
Karen Ward, Development Officer
Kirsteen MacRury, Grants and Finance Officer

Advisory Panel
Alistair Colquhoun, The Royal Bank of Scotland
Sebastian Conran, Sebastian Conran Associates
Paul Copland, Scottish Design Ltd
Simon Paterson, Paterson Brand Consultancy
Deyan Sudjic, Director, Glasgow 1999: UK City of Architecture and Design
Tim Wilkinson, Synthesis Consulting Ltd
Professor James Woudhuysen, Seymour Powell Associates

Acknowledgements
Glasgow Development Agency
Glasgow City Council
The Royal Bank of Scotland
Scottish Design Limited
Scottish Enterprise
Scottish Trade International
Glasgow Design Enterprise
Glasgow Opportunities
Glasgow Design Initiative
Design Council
The Lighthouse
British European Design Group
Glasgow School of Art
Department of Trade and Industry
British Embassy Vienna
British Embassy Paris
British Consulate-General Johannesburg
The British Council
Alasdair Smith
Neil Ramsey
Carole Friel
Bluepeach
McKeown Alexander Architects
Pure Design Limited
Scott Associates
The Lighting Association
FIRA (Furniture Industry Research Association)
Murgitroyd and Company